Freer Trade,
Protected
Environment

Freer Trade, Protected Environment

Balancing Trade Liberalization and Environmental Interests

C. Ford Runge

with François Ortalo-Magné and
Philip Vande Kamp

COUNCIL ON FOREIGN RELATIONS PRESS
NEW YORK

COUNCIL ON FOREIGN RELATIONS BOOKS

The Council on Foreign Relations, Inc., is a nonprofit and nonpartisan organization devoted to promoting improved understanding of international affairs through the free exchange of ideas. The Council does not take any position on questions of foreign policy and has no affiliation with, and receives no funding from, the United States government.

From time to time, books and monographs written by members of the Council's research staff or visiting fellows, or commissioned by the Council, or written by an independent author with critical review contributed by a Council study or working group are published with the designation "Council on Foreign Relations Book." Any book or monograph bearing that designation is, in the judgment of the Committee on Studies of the Council's Board of Directors, a responsible treatment of a significant international topic worthy of presentation to the public. All statements of fact and expressions of opinion contained in Council books are, however, the sole responsibility of the author.

If you would like more information on Council publications, please write the Council on Foreign Relations, 58 East 68th Street, New York, NY 10021, or call the Publications Office at (212) 734-0400.

Copyright © 1994 by the Council on Foreign Relations®, Inc.
All rights reserved.
Printed in the United States of America.

This book may not be reproduced, in whole or in part, in any form (beyond that copying permitted by Sections 107 and 108 of the U.S. Copyright Law and excerpts by reviewers for the public press), without written permission from the publishers. For information, write Publications Office, Council on Foreign Relations, 58 East 68th Street, New York, NY 10021.

Library of Congress Cataloging-in-Publication Data

Runge, C. Ford (Carlisle Ford)
    Freer trade, protected environment : balancing trade liberalization and environmental interests / C. Ford Runge.
        p.   cm.
    Includes bibliographical references and index.
    ISBN 0-87609-154-0 (pbk.) : $17.95
    1. Free trade—Environmental aspects.   2. Protectionism—Environmental aspects.   3. Environmental protection—International cooperation.   4. Environmental policy.   I Title.
HF1713.R86   1993
363.7—dc20
                                                            93-11315
                                                            CIP

94   95   96   97   98   EB   10   9   8   7   6   5   4   3   2   1

Cover design: Michael Storrings

Contents

In memory of Carlisle P. Runge
—soldier, lawyer, environmentalist

Foreword

Since mid-1992, a group of environmental and trade policy experts have met under the aegis of the Council on Foreign Relations in an attempt to bridge the gap between the environmental and trade disciplines—a gap that has exploded onto the world's trade, environmental, and political scenes in this decade. The group's objective was simple—to educate each other. There was no commitment to reach a consensus because this group was not formed to make recommendations.

We met eight times, including sessions in Minneapolis, Austin, and Seattle. These "field trips" were designed to address trade and environment concerns endemic to each of those three geographic areas. In Minneapolis, we examined the trade and environment aspects of agriculture; in Austin, the impact of NAFTA on the two disciplines; and in Seattle, trade and environment problems relating to fisheries and forestry. Our four New York sessions usually dealt in more "macro" terms, where fundamental issues and views were aired and discussed, led by two or more panelists who are recognized experts in their particular areas.

At the outset, we agreed that C. Ford Runge would write a monograph "on his own responsibility"—as the diplomats say—highlighting and addressing some of the key issues that sprang from the eight working sessions. Hence, Professor Runge's book should not be viewed as a consensus document or even the view of any particular member; whatever recommendations are brought forward in the text are his alone.

The preceding caveat should not, however, be construed as a washing of the group's hands. Rather, we recognized early on that no one person within the group could possibly reconcile all the different and sometimes disparate views of its members. The fundamental purpose of this book is to educate—here are some issues, here are various points of view dealing with each issue, and here are some possible "ways out."

The final chapters of the ongoing trade-environment debate have not been written. Indeed, one could argue with some credibility that the *first* chapters have hardly been written. As with many issues with political overtones, emotions run high. There is, for example no one more didactic than a true believer in free trade, unless it is a true believer in the environmental cause. Believers on both sides operate from a standard of purity, or at least a self-bestowed standard of purity.

But the real world is not pure, nor are there in most cases simple black and white choices. Such is the dilemma of the trade-environment debate. Neither side can win all the victories, and most of the victories—whoever wins—won't be clear-cut. Accommodation will have to be the rule if we are to have both a better trading system and a better environment.

Before we can arrive at even that reasonably happy state, however, we must be educated in the issues and problems besetting both the free-traders and the environmentalists, to understand history, and to appreciate different cultures and mores. One person's beautiful forest to enjoy and view is often another person's livelihood, and what is seen in the Northern hemisphere as worthy of being kept and cherished, is often viewed in the Southern hemisphere as the only chance to exit from wrenching poverty.

Above all, politicians have to be educated, because governments enact laws and regulations governing trade and the environment. The choices they face in the legislative process are no easier or less complicated than the issues this book examines, and politicians usually have far less time to think about them.

It is easy to say that the debate between traders and environmentalists is simply over jobs or rising standards of living, or between those who want to move forward and those who want the world to stand still. Such characterizations would grossly misrepresent the views of the majority of proponents on each side. As a member of the trading community, I like to consider myself also an environmentalist, and I believe the environmental members of our group support as strongly as I a more prosperous world community—a prosperity that trade brings.

Inevitably, compromises will have to be struck in the trade-environment debate, and, as in all of life, the art will be how and where to strike those compromises. This book only hints at those compromises, its primary focus being, as I have emphasized, to *educate*.

It is my hope that the Council study group will continue, for we are agreed on one thing: even our own education in this complex debate is barely at the elementary level; we have learned much from one another already, but we need to go on to "high school" and "college." As we do, we will share what we have learned with our readers, hopeful that they too will benefit from the learning process we are experiencing. This book is a long-overdue beginning to that process.

Michael S. Smith
Washington, D.C
January 1994

Preface

This study is a collective undertaking but an individual responsibility. It results from the Study Group on Trade and the Environment, organized during 1992–1993 at the Council on Foreign Relations in New York by C. Michael Aho, director of Economic Studies at the Council, and C. Ford Runge of the University of Minnesota. The study group was chaired by Ambassador Michael B. Smith, and was composed of a wide cross section of interested professionals from both the environmental and the trade communities. The group held five meetings in New York and three regional meetings (in Minneapolis, Austin, and Seattle) between June 1992 and May 1993.

Each meeting involved brief presentations by study group members, followed by a spirited discussion. (Appendices B and C contain, respectively, meeting agendas and a list of participants.) The observations and suggestions offered at the meetings provided the raw material for this book; but despite the critical role of the study group, the responsibility for these pages is the author's alone.

It is important to emphasize that this book does not attempt a complete accounting of all the issues involved in the trade and environment discussion, nor is it an attempt to steer a middle course through the opinions of the study group. Many of the participants have technical competence in specific areas beyond those of the authors; we do not intend a highly specialized or technical account.

This is a general analysis written for the informed layperson. Several excellent studies on the subject served as background for the discussions, and can be fruitfully studied in addition to this one. These include the U.S. Congress, Office of Technology Assessment, volume *Trade and Environment: Conflicts and Opportunities* (1992); the World Bank's collection of papers *International Trade and the Environment*, edited by Patrick Low (1992); and the papers contained in the General Agreement on Tariffs and Trade volume *The Greening of World Trade Issues* (1992), edited by Kym Anderson and Richard Blackhurst, and published by the University of Michigan.

Financial support for the study group was provided by the Cargill Foundation and Northwest Area Foundation of Minneapolis and St. Paul, and by the Council on Foreign Relations. In addition to all of the study group members, special thanks are due to my research assistants and co-authors François Ortalo-Magné and Philip Vande Kamp, and my executive secretary, Judy Berdahl. I would also like to thank C. Michael Aho, Marcia Aronoff, Stanley Barer, Lee Berlin, Lorrie Bodi, Michael Bonsignore, Steve Charnovitz, Willard W. Cochrane, William Diebold, Eli Whitney Debevoise II, Peter Emerson, Lynn Endicott, Daniel Esty, Mike Fitzgerald, Prudence Fox, Heidi Gifford, Gene Grossman, Annette Higby, Robert Housman, Robert Hudec, Stewart Hudson, John H. Jackson, Robbin Johnson, Ron Kramer, Ron Kroese, Marc Levinson, Bruce Lippke, Patrick Low, Katherine Mardirosian, Ray Mikesell, Stephen Mumme, Richard Nafziger, Wally Percyra, Jan Gilbreath Rich, Melanie Rowland, Mike Smith, Amy Solomon, Paul Sommers, Karl Stauber, Alison Von Klemperer, Konrad von Moltke, Justin Ward, Sidney Weintraub, Robert Weissler, John Whalley, and Gary Williams. To all of these people I owe much and am grateful.

C. Ford Runge
Saint Paul,
January 1994

Chapter 1

Trade and the Environment: Sabotage or Solution?

"SABOTAGE! of America's Health, Food Safety, and Environmental Laws," read the dramatic full-page ads in the *Washington Post* and *New York Times*, attacking the North American Free Trade Agreement (NAFTA) and the world trading organization, the General Agreement on Tariffs and Trade (GATT). The ads continued:

> . . . the only thing free about free trade is the freedom it gives the world's largest corporations to circumvent democracy and kill those local and national laws that protect people and the planet.

Both sovereignty and the environment were apparently at stake:

> In the present GATT talks called the *Uruguay Round*, new trade rules may soon give foreign governments the ability to challenge U.S. (and other democracies') laws as "barriers" to free trade . . . these new sets of trade rules . . . could be used against *thousands* of laws . . . that give priority to clean food and clean water, protect sea mammals and wildlife, preserve trees or other resources, restrict poisonous pesticide sprays, save rain forests and safeguard small farmers from being overpowered by agribusiness.[1]

These powerful charges, which first appeared early in 1992, were backed by powerful interests. The $50,000-ad was signed by a coalition of labor and environmental groups, including the Fair Trade Campaign, the Sierra Club, Ralph Nader's Public Citizen,

1

and the Center for International Environmental Law, all urging individuals to write to members of Congress opposing NAFTA and GATT.

While millions saw the ads, many fewer noted that a few months later Consumers Union, the respected publisher of *Consumer Reports*, issued a point-by-point rebuttal, noting that the ads "relied heavily on inaccurate statements of fact, on inapt analogies . . . on misconstructions or highly debatable constructions of the text of the current Uruguay Round proposal, and on a factually unsupported theory of a conspiracy between multinational businesses and international organizations." Commenting that trade and trade agreements constitute an important instrument by which developing nations can compete in world markets with larger nations, thus improving their standards of living (and hence their environment), Consumers Union also observed that the use of GATT to challenge domestic policies suspected of serving as trade barriers is a power that "has existed and been used by other governments (and the U.S. against foreign laws) since the 1947 agreement. Along with equalizing and reducing tariffs, this reduction of non-tariff trade barriers is an overriding purpose of the Agreement."[2]

Who is right? Is trade liberalization likely to harm the environment, or is trade part of the solution? What role do international organizations such as GATT, and agreements such as NAFTA, play in this struggle? Sorting through these and other issues in the trade-environment debate is not simple. Motives and methods are often not what they appear. Trade and its links to the environment are hotly debated and highly politicized, and claims and counterclaims are often exaggerated by those with narrow interests. In July 1993, for example, several environmental groups (who had also signed the SABOTAGE! ad) won a suit in federal court demanding an environmental impact assessment of NAFTA. The Clinton administration immediately gave notice of intent to appeal, and the issue seemed headed for the Supreme Court. Was this because the Clinton White House was opposed to an environmental assessment of NAFTA, or simply because it found the highly formalized assessment process an inappropriate tool in the development of trade policy? This and other such issues require more than superficial assertions.

As debates over trade and environment rage in and outside of Washington, a need exists to sift through the hyperbole and counterclaims and to assess the reality. In pursuit of this goal, the Council on Foreign Relations founded the Study Group on Trade and the Environment in mid-1992. In its membership were representatives of many environmental groups—including the Environmental Defense Fund, National Wildlife Federation, Natural Resources Defense Council, and Sierra Club—as well as representatives from the trade, business, and academic communities (listed in appendix C). At a series of nine meetings, the group sought opinions and guidance from both environmentalists and trade experts.

What emerged was a classic conflict of cultures, in which the worlds of environmentalists and trade experts collided head-on. The experience was jolting. Most traders took it almost on faith that more trade was preferred to less. Their reasons: the role of protectionism in fueling the Depression of the 1930s, the growth of incomes and jobs created by trade since World War II, and the fact that such growth seemed a precondition for environmental protection. Many environmentalists, in contrast, viewed such growth, if unaccompanied by strict environmental regulation, as part of the problem rather than the solution. Environmentalists saw the unregulated growth of the postwar period as largely responsible for the despoliation of the world's resources. Some questioned the benefits of economic growth itself. Traders, meanwhile, were deeply suspicious that many environmental claims against trade were simply protectionism in "green" disguise.

Fueling this mutual distrust were complex legal questions affecting both trade and the environment, in which the worst suspicions of both camps seemed confirmed. In 1991, for example, a GATT panel issued a report critical of U.S. laws designed to protect marine mammals, especially dolphins, from injury in tuna fishing nets. U.S. law provided for trade sanctions against noncomplying countries to enforce the regulations. The trade sanctions were found in violation of GATT, confirming environmentalists' worst fears: that GATT placed trade interests above the environment in a hierarchy of values.

From the trade side, meanwhile, environmental groups seemed to place the environment uncompromisingly above all else, while often allying themselves with opponents of more liberal trade in the debate over GATT and NAFTA. In the case of NAFTA, some environmentalists argued that more open trade would turn Mexico into an environmental dumping ground. Traders countered that Mexico's environmental problems, while serious, could be met only if Mexico's economy could grow sufficiently to allow needed investment in environmental protection. Keeping Mexico poor was no solution.

The presidential campaign of 1992, while hardly a referendum on trade policy, initiated Ross Perot's critique of NAFTA as a suction for U.S. jobs. Candidate Clinton conditioned his support of NAFTA on calls for new environmental and labor safeguards. The result was the August 1993 negotiation by U.S. Trade Representative Mickey Kantor of new environmental and labor "side agreements" to the NAFTA text. Environmental concerns, in other words, are now a central element in trade reforms.

The stakes in the trade-environment debate are enormous. They involve nothing less than the future of both the world trading system and the global environment. Whether trading nations can pursue growth through trade with sufficient environmental safeguards to protect the globe from widespread environmental destruction, and how current and new institutions, at both the domestic and the international levels, can be strengthened for this purpose, will largely determine the outcome.

How did the collision of trade and environment occur, and why now? In the 1980s and 1990s, air pollution, acid rain, and global warming became major items on the international agenda as environmental issues moved beyond domestic policy. This shift reflected growing recognition of the global impact of economic development and the rising problem of international environmental hazards that spill over national borders and affect the oceans, air, climate, and biological resources of the planet. Just as environmental risks flow through the world's biosphere, so they flow through the world economy—and threaten to disrupt it. Some regulatory differences exist among countries at the same stage of development, but in the world as a whole the major differences in environmental and health regulations run along a divide between the developed North and the developing nations of the South. Across this divide in regulation flows trade.

At the same time, growing consumer concerns about environmental quality and pollution in the North were prompting more attention to environmental hazards from imported products, particularly food. The European Community (EC), now the European Union (EU), for example, banned beef imports of cattle treated with certain hormones, triggering a continuing trade dispute with the United States. In the EU, North America, and Japan, domestic interests and other producers seeking protection from foreign competition were finding a new source of support in the environmental movement. Import restrictions, when presented as a public health measure, gained a legitimacy that they might not otherwise enjoy.

These events suggest the new realities that uneven environmental and health regulation and their links to trade create. When nations exchange goods and services, they also trade environmental and health risks. These risks accompany the goods and services traded across national borders, and have emerged as a major source of tension in trade negotiations. The United States and other GATT signatories are committed to pursuing more open borders in the ongoing Uruguay Round of trade negotiations. But as national health, safety, and environmental regulations grow in importance, different national regulatory priorities create serious frictions for trade and development strategies. These frictions were especially obvious in negotiations over NAFTA.

Who are the players, and what are their views in this collision of worldviews? On the environmental side, nearly every major interest group has taken a position. Many have tended to support trade reforms on the condition that environmental safeguards and assessments accompany them; some, however, have remained bitterly opposed to any of the proposed safeguards and to trade reform itself. Trade and business interests have slowly—perhaps too slowly—come to recognize the importance of (and the political support enjoyed by) environmental groups, and to demand discussions of ways to integrate environmental concerns into trade reform. Overall, the *environmental* community generally sees risks in more open trade, while the *trade* community sees threats to economic growth and integration if environmental concerns lead to barriers to trade. Advocates of more open trade and environmentalists alike share concerns over how global environmental and trade agreements are to be linked, whether one or the other should take precedence, and the methods by which conflicts should be resolved. Yet the conflict of cultures and collision of interests, far from being over, has really only begun.

The collision of trade and the environment has produced a critical need for careful and balanced, if not disinterested, assessment of these issues and the challenges they pose for policymakers. The increasingly competitive and often acrimonious trade relations between the United States, the EU, and Japan are one institutional axis along which trade and environmental issues arise. Despite the similarities among the developed countries of the North, they have differences not only in scientific and environmental standards, but in culture and social norms, that will continually confound efforts to harmonize environmental regulations. Challenges to these regulations such as nontariff trade barriers—both within regional trade blocs (for example the EU) and between nations (for instance, the United States, Japan, and Canada)—are likely to be recurrent themes.

The gap between the environmental regulations along the North-South axis is even wider, accentuating institutional problems of harmonization and concerns over "pollution havens" and competitiveness. The NAFTA negotiations reflect these differences in microcosm, with Mexico attempting rapidly to upgrade its environmental regulations in order to satisfy fears in the United States and Canada. From the perspective of the North, fears include lower costs of environmental compliance by competitors in the South; movement of firms and industries into these low-regulation areas; import of goods (such as fruits and vegetables) tainted by treatments banned in the North for environmental reasons; and use of production methods in the South objectionable to environmental interests. From the perspective of many in the South, the environmental regulations adopted in the North, even if desirable, may be unaffordable. In addition, many developing countries suspect the North of using its higher standards to discriminate against products and processes primarily for trade rather than environmental reasons.

THE BOOK IN OVERVIEW

The purpose of this book is to create an island in this stream of public discussion and debate, designed for an audience of interested but nonexpert readers. Its underlying premise is that environmental and trade policies are *equally important* to the welfare of U.S. and foreign citizens, and deserve to be considered on equal terms. Trade and environmental interests can often be pursued jointly, in a manner that protects the benefits that expanded trade can bring, while ensuring that these benefits do not come at the expense of the environment. Finding areas of complementarity is a difficult balancing act. Different circumstances will imply different priorities attached to trade and environmental interests. If a new doctrine is expressed in this study, it is the *doctrine of balance* between trade and the environment.

The chapters to follow are organized to provide first a framework for understanding linkages from trade to the environment, then take up real cases and focus on some of the main issues in the debate, and finally develop the lessons of these cases and examine the policy implications. Chapter 2 attempts to put the debate in a legal, economic, and environmental framework, giving depth and rigor to the arguments involved. Comparing legal and economic approaches, while integrating environmental concerns, provides a basic understanding of the criteria that can guide future policy choices. Chapter 3 takes up the most politically salient issue: that trade liberalization will lead to increased levels of environmental damages. The main issue addressed in chapter 4 is the question of "disguised protectionism." The fundamental issue concerns the ability to distinguish legitimate environmental measures, which may well distort trade, from those that not only are trade-distorting but have little basis from an environmental standpoint. Chapter 5 takes up the relationship between trade agreements and environmental agreements, using the example of the Montreal Protocol, aimed at protecting atmospheric ozone. Finally, chapter 6 develops some of these lessons, and recommends a variety of critical steps for

U.S. policymakers and the international community. Several radically new environmental institutions are proposed at the international level, together with a call for fuller public participation in and government attention to the emerging trade-environment nexus. One overriding point is clear: The United States must exercise leadership in the development and implementation of these new institutions. It is in the self-interest of the United States, as one of the major trading economies in the world, and as a world leader in environmental protection, to implement new policies to navigate the crosscurrents created by the confluence of trade and the environment.

Chapter 2

Understanding Environment and Trade Linkages: Legal, Economic, and Environmental Perspectives

While the debate over trade and environment is multifaceted, three main perspectives dominate the discussion. The first is a *legal* perspective, in which environmental rules and standards are compared with trade rules in order to define and assign responsibility for national and international actions. GATT and NAFTA are first and foremost a set of legal rules. The legal approach compares trade rules and environmental standards and the burdens imposed by each. When a nation develops an environmental standard such as a ban on products containing certain polluting chemicals, this may place a burden on those importing such products from overseas, and may act to protect domestic producers. Is this burden or protection justified by the environmental harm that it avoids? How are such justifications to be measured? What body or group should decide such questions? These are largely questions of law, both domestic and international.

These legal rules define *economic* obligations. A second approach to trade and environment is thus an economic one. What are the economic consequences of environmental damages resulting from unregulated trade? If trade is restricted for environmental

9

reasons, what harm is done to consumers and producers of goods and services at home and abroad? How can the environmental harm be mitigated at least cost in terms of trade distortion, and how can trade be expanded at least cost to the environment? An economic approach estimates and evaluates these impacts of trade measures on the environment, and of environmental measures on trade.

The third perspective, often lacking from both purely legal and economic discussions, is the *environmental* one, in which the main focus is on ecological impacts. Each perspective provides important insights, and merits separate attention. When legal and economic analyses give appropriate weight to the environment, the need to reorganize national and international policies becomes more clear. Let us begin by thinking through how each perspective influences the trade-environment debate.

LEGAL PERSPECTIVES

Both environmental and trade rules are legal instruments that regulate the actions of individuals, firms, and governments in the conduct of commerce. Environment and trade intersect when trade actions lead to claims of environmental harm, or when environmental standards lead to claims of trade harm, or when international trade and environmental rules appear mutually inconsistent or ambiguous. Fortunately, in many cases, environmental and trade rules do not intersect at all, and there is no claim of harm, inconsistency, or ambiguity. But the increasingly integrated global marketplace, combined with a rising awareness of environmental damages due to market activity, has led to a growing number of such conflicts.

Trade Measures and Environmental Damages

The linkages from trade to the environment are complex. In many respects, trade promotes more efficient uses of natural resources, reducing wasteful patterns of production and consumption. But trade distortions and the simple volume and scale of trading activity may also result in environmental damages.

In seeking to reduce internal barriers to trade, the EU creates additional flows of goods and services, but may also increase the flows of "bads" and disservices, such as pollution from higher levels of automobile and truck traffic. NAFTA poses similar challenges, with fears over water and air pollution in the border region and the possible influx into the United States and Canada of products that fail to meet domestic health and environmental standards. Yet potential environmental burdens arise not just from changes in trade rules that *open* access to markets, and may actually be made worse from trade rule changes that *close* access or guarantee protected or differential access.

Protectionism, in short, does not guarantee reductions in environmental hazards, and may even exacerbate such problems. An example, considered in more detail below, is the convention that provides special access to the EU for animal feeds based on manioc (tapioca): this convention, together with the protectionism and price supports characteristic of European agricultural policy, have encouraged expansion in polluting livestock facilities in the Netherlands. Other examples are export bans on tropical hardwood timber that have lowered domestic timber prices in countries such as Ecuador, discouraging conservation and encouraging unsustainable rates of cutting.[1]

An important question also is whether trade is the true culprit. While trade may amplify and aggravate damages, it can also promote more efficient resource use. If the benefits of trade are accompanied by enforced regulation that reduces or eliminates these damages, then its burdens have been "internalized"and its benefits remain. In some cases, damaging environmental consequences of trade and development are difficult to avoid, even with strict regulation. Export-oriented intensive agricultural production in the heartland of North America, for example, is responsible for a substantial amount of water pollution in the United States.[2] Even if agricultural production were more strictly regulated, some damage to soil and water resources would continue. Yet this production is a highly competitive trade sector in the North American economy, consistently contributing balance-of-trade surpluses to both the United States and Canada, and employing millions of full- and part-time farmers and food-sector workers. The burden imposed on the environment is thus offset at some level by these trade benefits. While some might argue that no environmental burdens are tolerable or justified, trade-offs must and will be made: slightly less agricultural output in return for cleaner water; slightly more erosion in return for farm exports and income. Striking a balance between trade and the environment requires a careful assessment of these impacts and the cost of minimizing damages, and recognition of the fact that additional environmental regulations may be necessary. Fundamentally, this is a matter of offsetting damages linked to trade by imposing some type of regulation, including changes in economic incentives though taxes, subsidies, or fees.

A more complicated issue arises when trade is linked to environmental damages, but the damages occur outside the home market, beyond the reach of domestic laws. Such was the case in the "tuna-dolphin" dispute (see chapter 4), when the United States imposed trade embargoes to enforce laws designed to prevent dolphin kills in fishing nets used to catch tuna in foreign waters. In such cases, regulation takes on international legal significance, and questions of jurisdiction and sovereignty arise.

Whether the trade measure has its primary environmental impact at home, abroad, or in the "global commons" (such as the atmospheric ozone layer), a decision must be arrived at to take action in response. This process, admittedly somewhat oversimplified, is shown schematically in Figure 1. A trade measure (for instance, an export ban or market integration process, such as

FIGURE 1.   ENVIRONMENTAL AND REGULATORY IMPLICATIONS
OF TRADE MEASURES

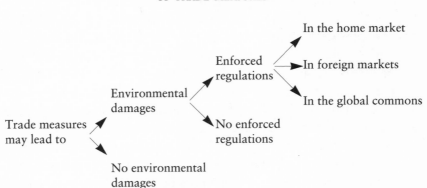

NAFTA) may lead to environmental damages (or it may not). If damages occur and are to be offset, then either the trade measure itself must be changed, or some type of regulatory response (for example, taxes or subsidies) must be implemented and enforced. The venue for this implementation and enforcement may be the home market, foreign markets, or even the global commons, as in the case of the atmospheric ozone layer. The wider the scope of intervention, the more legally complex issues of jurisdiction and sovereignty become.

Once a linkage from trade measures to environmental damages is established, the next issue is how best to respond. In the United States, an often-employed response in the domestic sphere is the environmental impact statement (EIS) procedure under the National Environmental Policy Act of 1969.[3] This procedure is applied to major federal actions, and involves detailed environmental assessments, often leading federal agencies to additional actions, including regulations, required to protect the environment. In many cases, the preparation of the statement itself reassures those who fear potentially adverse environmental consequences. If the damages occur outside the home market, or as part of the global commons, then environmental impact assessments may still occur, but their capacity to force regulatory responses is more limited.

The appropriateness of an EIS in cases of trade agreements is at issue in NAFTA. Several organizations, including the Sierra Club, Public Citizen, and Friends of the Earth, urged an EIS for NAFTA as early as 1991. On June 30, 1993, the U.S. District Court ruled in their behalf against the U.S. Trade Representative. The latter immediately indicated its intention to appeal the decision, arguing that NAFTA is not covered by the requirements of the National Environmental Policy Act, which requires an EIS for "every recommendation or report on proposals for legislation and other Federal actions significantly affecting the quality of the human environment." Although NAFTA certainly requires implementing legislation, the Clinton administration argued that presidential actions do not require an EIS review, and that NAFTA is primarily a presidential action, with the Trade Representative playing only an advisory function.[4] In a brief filed in August 1993, several other environmental groups proposed a more rapid process for an EIS, using a special and expedited review in which existing data can be assembled within a few months.[5] Regardless of the outcome, which is likely to end in the Supreme Court, the Clinton administration acknowledged the important environmental questions of NAFTA, but questioned whether an EIS is the way to achieve an appropriate review.

It is worth noting that some trade actions appear to cause no obvious environmental damages; it would therefore be gratuitous and wasteful to propose that all trade be subjected to environmental assessments. If, for example, the United States were to change textile quotas, allowing foreign shipments of additional blue jeans into the domestic market, it would be hard to make a case for an environmental assessment in the home (U.S.) market. Yet where a legal case can be made for linkage from trade measures to environmental damages, and the level of these damages and the appropriate response are in doubt, such an assessment can provide useful information. The danger in calling for full-scale assessments of *all* trade actions is that the assessments will appear to (and in fact will) obstruct the expansion of trade, lending credence to the view that environmental claims are substituting for protectionism. It is noteworthy that those environmental groups filing suit against the Trade Representative and demanding an EIS were outspoken in their opposition to NAFTA.

It is also doubtful whether the environmental assessment process, which has been applied to specific projects (such as dams and other water diversions) and various U.S. regulations, is equally well suited to trade agreements covering many products and multiple sectors of the economy. A well-defined baseline, or "no-build," alternative exists for a dam or water diversion, but is absent for a trade agreement, such as NAFTA. The larger and more complex the trade measure, the more unwieldy and general in focus an EIS will become. For example, environmental groups criticized the Bush administration's environmental assessment of the impacts of NAFTA on the U.S.-Mexico border because of its overly general and conjectural nature.[6] If full-blown environmental assessments of NAFTA and other trade measures *are* undertaken, the more specifically focused they are, the more useful they will be as instruments in the design of needed environmental safeguards.

Environmental Measures and Trade Burdens

When domestic environmental measures lead to claims of *trade harm*, it is generally because a burden has been imposed on individuals or firms seeking to export or import goods or services in the name of domestic (and sometimes global) environmental protection. The balancing question now is whether the environmental measure is justified primarily as a form of needed environmental protection or is a disguised restriction to trade, in which harmful trade effects offset beneficial environmental effects. Here again, a trade-off judgment must be made concerning the costs (due to trade distortion) that should be borne in order to protect the environment.

Currently in such cases, the environmental measures may conflict with GATT rules that call for "national treatment"—that is, treatment of foreign goods in a manner "no less favourable than accorded to like products of national origin." Interpreting the concept of national treatment as it relates to the environment is made more difficult by the fact that differences in natural conditions in various countries can cause the same treatment of the "same" products to have very different ecological consequences, as in the case of timber harvesting in especially fragile ecosystems. Environmental restrictions with effects on trade may also potentially fall afoul of GATT prohibitions against "unnecessary obstacles to international trade." However, GATT grants certain exceptions for the "conservation of exhaustible resources" and human health and safety. It is the interplay between general attempts to promote national treatment and to reduce protectionism, and the recognition that exceptions for the environment will be needed, that stands at the center of the trade-environment debate.[7]

These issues are not new to students of U.S. or European economic history. Whether a government environmental regulation is a nontariff trade barrier is a question faced domestically in the United States by the states under the Commerce Clause of the U.S. Constitution, and by the twelve member states in the EU under the EU treaties, accession agreements, and the Single European Act. As Robert Hudec and Daniel Farber of the University of Minnesota

Law faculty argue, such questions typically break down into two parts: Does the measure create a burden on trade? Is the burden justified by the environmental benefits of the regulation?[8]

From a legal perspective the apparent burden imposed on trade is a "gateway concept." The presence of an apparent burden opens the way to further inquiry as to a measure's justification, in which its benefits for the environment are weighed against its harm to trade. If no burden is found, then the trade effects of the regulation are not at issue. The process shown in Figure 2 (again, somewhat oversimplified) is thus analogous to that shown above in Figure 1. An environmental measure may be linked to trade distortion (or it may not). If this distortion imposes a burden on trade, then it may still be justified in the name of environmental protection. How it is justified depends on a number of legal issues related to specific elements of GATT.

Let us briefly review this process, starting at the lefthand side of Figure 2. First is the linkage from environmental regulations to trade burdens. While nearly all environmental regulations impose different burdens on commercial transactions by different firms, to be trade-related this difference must exist between foreign producers and their domestic competition. This differential may be relatively easy to see, as when foreign products are subjected to

FIGURE 2.   TRADE IMPLICATIONS OF ENVIRONMENTAL MEASURES

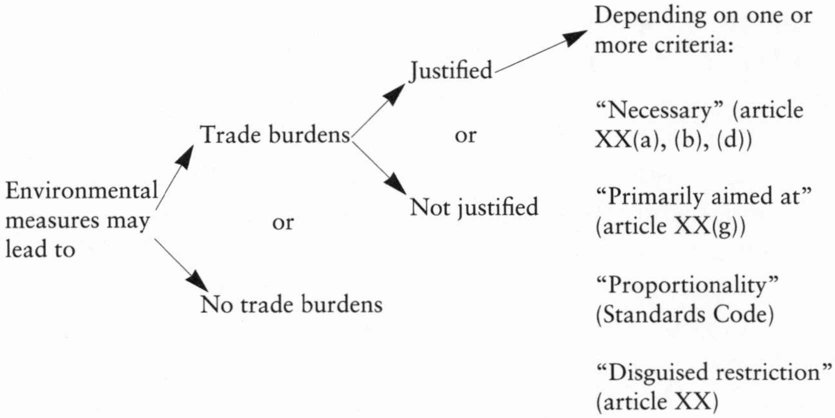

obviously different standards than are domestic products. Under section 337 of the 1930 Trade Act, for example, the International Trade Commission (ITC) hears certain trade cases for foreign violators, while U.S. courts hear cases against U.S. firms charged with similar violations. In general, going before the ITC is regarded as more burdensome to the defendant. Not every differential rule clearly constitutes a burden, however, even though domestic and foreign products are treated differently. Inspections of auto safety glass at U.S. auto manufacturers' factories are different from inspections of foreign vehicles' windshields at the border, but the border inspections do not appear to create a differential burden.

Less obvious are standards that appear neutral on their face, but have a differential impact on foreign and domestic products. Provisions of the 1985 Farm Bill sought to apply sanitary processing and inspection standards to chicken from outside the United States that were "the same" as the standards used domestically. (The phrase "the same" was substituted for previous language calling for foreign standards "at least equal to" those used domestically at the request of members of Congress from Arkansas.) In a case brought before the federal court for the Southern District of Mississippi, the language calling for "the same" standard was upheld, despite warnings from the Department of Agriculture that "such a definitional finding would augur dire foreign trade implications."[9]

Similar types of "burden" questions arise in the context of the EU. Since 1989, the twelve nations of the EU and the United States have engaged in a continuing dispute over an EU regulation banning the sale of beef treated with supplementary growth hormones, whether the beef was raised inside or out of Europe. The United States alleged this action to be a disguised barrier to trade, but the EU defended it as necessary to protect a perceived risk to consumers' health and safety. The matter has not been finally resolved.

In both the "safe chicken" and the "beef hormones" cases, a domestic regulation had a differential effect on foreign competitors, not because foreigners were subjected to different standards, but because conforming to a new domestic regulation would require retooling and restarting a foreign production method. However, simply finding that such an effect is burdensome may be too wide a "gateway," leading to a presumed need to justify almost every impact of domestic environmental regulations on trade, creating a chilling effect on such regulatory oversight.

Such an "open gate" is analogous on the trade side to the argument on the environmental side that virtually every trade measure should be subjected to an environmental assessment. This is a part of the reason many trade reformers argue for "harmonization" of standards or, alternatively, that the same results be achieved by equivalent regulatory means, so that differences in national regulations can be tolerated. Environmental critics have charged, however, that too much leeway, combined with a drive to harmonize regulations, can propel the global structure of regulation toward a "lowest common denominator."[10]

Supposing that a burden to trade appears to be due to an environmental measure, a second issue arises: How can this be justified in terms of environmental protection? Several justifications exist under GATT, all of which amount to attempts to balance the environmental benefits of the measure (or its benefits for health and safety) against the harm it does to trade. The first and simplest test is the "necessary" test.[11] "Necessity," in this context, means that the goal cannot be realistically accomplished by means that are less burdensome to trade. Related to this judgment is the question of how the objective of the domestic regulation is framed. In the "safe chicken" case, is the objective to achieve exactly identical processing methods, or simply to guarantee food safety? If it is the former, then only "the same" processing standards will suffice; if the latter, then it is less clear that "the same" standards are "necessary" to achieve food safety. As Robert Hudec has argued, whether a burdensome regulation is "necessary" to achieve a domestic environmental or health and safety objective "is really an interlocking decision about whether, as compared with the next least restrictive alternative, the extra burden is worth the extra gain."[12]

A second legal test applied to environmental measures has been the "primarily aimed at" test.[13] Is the environmental measure "primarily aimed at" conservation, and not at some other (presumably protectionist) objective? In a case heard before both a GATT dispute resolution panel and a Canada-U.S. Free Trade Agreement (FTA) panel (discussed in chapter 4), the required landing of 100 percent of U.S. salmon and herring catch to be counted for "conservation" purposes was found to be invalid. The panels concluded that the regulations were not primarily aimed at conservation. The FTA panel, in particular, reasoned that the Canadian government would not have imposed the regulation for conservation purposes if the full burden had fallen on Canadian citizens. Hence, given the legitimacy of the conservation goal (of preserving the salmon and herring fishery), the question of whether the environmental measure is "primarily aimed at" this goal reduces to whether the extra gain in environmental terms of counting 100 percent of the catch was worth the added burden on trade. In economic terms, the "primarily aimed at" test can be thought of in terms of cost-effectiveness: Is the trade-distorting measure (assuming that its goals are legitimate for conservation purposes) the most cost-effective way of protecting the environment, or are there more direct ways of doing the same thing that impose fewer burdens on trade?

A third test of whether the burden of environmental measures on trade is justified comes from the 1979 Standards Code, developed in the Tokyo Round of multilateral trade negotiations. This test is known as "proportionality."[14] Here, as in the "necessary" and "primarily aimed at" tests, a balance ("proportionality") is sought between the benefits of the environmental measure and its costs in terms of trade restriction. The environmental goals defined as legitimate are assumed, so the question reduces to whether the measure is "more trade restrictive than necessary" to reduce the risks "nonfulfillment would create."

A fourth test is the "disguised restriction" test.[15] In effect, it simply restates whether a measure is really protectionism "in disguise." In practice, this test differs little from the "primarily aimed at" test.

In summary, if an environmental measure imposes a burden on trade, whether the burden is justified can be assessed using several criteria. All appeal to the idea that if feasible alternatives exist that are less trade-distorting, but that still protect the environment, then they should be considered in lieu of existing measures. Who is to make these judgments, and how they are to be enforced, will be the subject of later chapters. For now, we seek only to clarify the nature of the judgments themselves.

Conflicts Between Trade and Environmental Rules

As the number of international environmental agreements has grown in recent years, new questions have arisen over the relationship between them and existing or future trade obligations in GATT.[16] First is the question of whether countries are *parties or nonparties* to the treaties, such as the Montreal Protocol, affecting chlorofluorocarbon (CFC) and halon emissions damaging to atmospheric ozone. The Montreal Protocol, signed in 1987 and amended by later agreements, commits the signatory parties to study the feasibility of a ban applied to nonmember countries against imports of products made with a process that uses ozone-depleting chemicals, as well as various other actions affecting trade in these products (see chapter 5). In January 1993, for example, signatories were scheduled to ban the export of these substances to nonparties.[17] However, fewer than twenty countries were signatories by 1992, whereas over a hundred countries are signatories to the GATT articles. If countries are parties to GATT, with all of the *trade* obligations that this implies, and are also parties to the Montreal Protocol and its amendments, with all of the *environmental* obligations this implies, then what if these obligations conflict? Alternatively, what if countries that have signed the Montreal Protocol take trade actions to ban imports from countries that have *not* signed the Protocol? Clearly, principles must be established to determine matters of priority and consistency.

In addition to the question of obligations under various treaties to which countries are pledged is the question of "extrajurisdictionality," or whether countries have rights to impose trade measures in response to the environmental policies of other countries. This issue has come to the forefront with the U.S.-Mexico tuna-dolphin dispute. Can the United States, under GATT, ban imports of tuna caught with fishing methods that kill dolphins in the process, even if these actions take effect outside the territorial jurisdiction of the United States?

A third question, related to the first two, is the legal standing of international environmental agreements versus GATT obligations. While the Vienna Convention on the Law of Treaties provides general rules on the relationship of successive treaties—notably, that the treaty "later in time" prevails[18]—the rule applies only where the two treaties address the same subject matter. In the case of a party to both the Montreal Protocol and GATT, for example, the section of the Protocol banning imports of substances produced with ozone-depleting chemicals would prevail over any inconsistent provisions of GATT (assuming the GATT articles are considered a treaty). While the "later in time" rule of the Vienna Convention allows subsequent environmental agreements to "trump" trade obligations, some feel it may make it too easy to override trade rules in the name of these objectives.[19] In cases in which a country is not a party to the environmental agreement, the Vienna Convention (article 34) states that the agreement that is later in time cannot bind nonparty states without their consent, unless the treaty rules become customary international law.[20]

A fourth issue affecting the relationship between international environmental agreements and trade obligations is whether multilateral agreements, such as the Montreal Protocol, are subject to the GATT exceptions for conservation of exhaustible natural resources. In the tuna-dolphin case, for example, the GATT panel suggested that the "necessity" of an action could be determined in part by whether the parties had at least tried to resolve their differences through an international agreement. If measures relating to the conservation of exhaustible natural resources are taken to include international agreements such as the Montreal Protocol, a question remains whether they apply only in the home countries' jurisdiction, or to the broader international setting, including the global commons. It is also unclear whether the implementation actions of such an agreement are also to be treated as exceptions under GATT.[21]

In response to this lack of definition and clarity, leading authorities (such as John Jackson of the University of Michigan Law School) have proposed a GATT "waiver" for international environmental agreements, at last until better definitions and understandings can be worked out.[22] A waiver limited to, say, five years might include specific current environmental agreements and provide for future ones as well. In addition to the Montreal Protocol, such a waiver might include the Convention on International Trade in Endangered Species of Wild Flora and Fauna,[23] and the Basel Convention on the Control of Transboundary Movements of Hazardous Wastes and Their Disposal.[24]

Even proponents of a waiver, such as Jackson, note that it fails to address a number of related questions. Should it apply only to trade measures *required* under an environmental agreement, or be extended to other measures that are discretionary but *authorized*, or even to unilateral trade actions designed to implement or enforce environmental measures? Steve Charnovitz observes that waivers are meant for exceptional circumstances, and that international environmental agreements are increasingly unexceptional.[25]

ECONOMIC PERSPECTIVES

What the legal rules affecting trade and the environment *affect* are trade flows of goods and services, including environmental "goods," such as air and water quality, and "bads," such as hazardous wastes. The analysis of these issues by economists began with Adam Smith. Since then, it has become commonplace to note that expanded trade brings benefits because it allows individuals and countries to specialize in those things that they do well and cheaply. Rather than everything being produced in the home market, some things can be produced more efficiently abroad, for which home goods can then be traded, to the benefit of all countries.

British political economist David Ricardo, writing in 1817, concisely expressed the abstract argument in favor of free trade.

> Under a system of perfectly free [international] commerce, each country naturally devotes its capital and labour to such employments as are most beneficial to each. This pursuit of individual advantage is admirably connected with the universal good of the whole. By stimulating industry, by rewarding ingenuity, and by using most efficaciously the peculiar powers bestowed by nature, it distributes labour most effectively and most economically: while, by increasing the general mass of productions, it diffuses general benefit.[26]

This argument, despite its intuitive appeal, is essentially a priori, and collides with a real world in which protectionism is rife. In this highly politicized real-world setting, appeals to abstract models are less persuasive than those to actual experience. On experiential grounds, however, the case for freer, more open trade (if not textbook "free trade") remains strong.

Substantial accumulated evidence indicates that economic welfare, measured conventionally by gross domestic product (GDP) per capita, has benefited significantly from more open trade since World War II. In the short period since 1985, U.S. exports to the rest of the world have doubled, and global incomes have increased by almost a fifth.[27] However, not all of this growth is due to freer trade; and the process of "opening," when it occurs, bears little relation to the free trade models of pure economic theory, since many imperfections and "market failures" remain that make such models unrealistic. Among the failures of the market are serious environmental damages. Most countries have concluded that economic growth requires attention to these damages.

It was not always so. Economists at one time defended the idea that those who "lost" in trade liberalization could be compensated subsequently out of the gains from trade, thus assuring "potential" welfare gains.[28] A version of this argument is that if environmental damages result from trade liberalization, then the gains from trade can be redirected to repair these damages. However, the theoretical argument that free trade is welfare-maximizing depends on the absence of damages, such as air or water pollution, that the market alone is generally incapable of correcting. Where such failures occur, the gains from trade are *not* assured; and even if liberalization yields welfare gains, they may be more than offset by environmental damages that lower welfare (see appendix A). Finally, how the gains and the losses from trade are distributed cannot be separated from the process of trade creation when environmental damages are present that destroy the informational function of prices.[29] Hence, even in theory, trade liberalization does not guarantee welfare improvements unless environmental damages are dealt with concomitantly.[30] Economic theory therefore provides no argument in favor of the priority of trade over the environment.

Yet many developing countries have noted that *without* increases in incomes, environmental quality improvements may be beyond reach. Referring to Mexican environmental pollution problems, analyst David Voigt notes that "while these problems are complex and diverse, they can all be traced to a common source. That source is the lack of economic resources available in Mexico to adequately control the environmental effects of development in the border region."[31] As a practical matter, therefore, it may not be possible for poor countries to increase incomes and reduce environmental damages at the same time: some lags may occur. In developed countries, by contrast, it is unlikely that trade liberalization can succeed, economically or politically, unless environmental objectives are considered jointly.

In general, however, economists believe that more trade is preferred to less, and that reciprocal reductions in the protection of home markets are therefore welfare-improving. This approach has dominated thinking in GATT, and has been the prevailing wisdom in efforts to liberalize trade in the postwar period. Naturally, the two-hundred-year-old-plus debate over trade benefits and protectionism involves many complex side arguments, especially concerning the utility of trade liberalization when home or foreign markets are already characterized by monopoly or other market failures. What was considered a side argument on environmental impacts of trade only a few years ago, however, has emerged as more central.

Market Failure and Environmental Damages

Environmental pollution as an example of market failure is generally characterized by economists as an "externality."[32] This term creates confusion and a certain suspicion among noneconomists and many environmentalists, because it seems to imply that pollution is "external" to the problems of market functioning, and therefore of secondary concern. This is not what is meant, however; to say that pollution and environmental degradation are "externalities" is simply to say that the market fails to account for their true costs, and that an accurate accounting of these costs would lead to lower estimates of the gains from trade. Environmental economists, in particular, devote the better part of their efforts to devising schemes to confront these market failures, either by regulating pollution directly or by creating "quasi-market" incentives, such as taxes or subsidies, which allow the true value of environmental benefits to be reflected in prices.

For example, it is widely held that the market price of petroleum fuels fails to reflect the costs of the damages these fuels do to the environment, including air pollution and oil spills at sea. One way to encourage conservation of petroleum and the development of alternatives is to impose a tax on oil and gas so that the true cost to society is better reflected in consumer and producer prices. However, if instead of such a tax, a tariff on oil imports or regulations prohibiting imports of foreign oil were imposed, it might be argued that an environmental measure was acting as a burden to trade. A determination of whether this burden is justified or not could then proceed according to the previous section: the environmental benefits of the oil import fee or import restriction would be weighed against its costs in the form of trade distortion.

Economists thus consider most environmental problems under a single rubric of "externality." But to say that something "is not accounted for" by the market is not to say much. At least three types of externalities are relevant to the trade and environment debate:

- those that have their origins and main impact in the home or domestic market, or "local externalities";

- those that have their origins in one market and their main impact in foreign markets following trade, or "transnational externalities";

- those that have impacts on many or even all countries, or "global externalities."

These types of externalities require different responses, and correspond to the venues of effects shown in Figure 1 (the home market, foreign markets, the global commons). An example of local externalities would be sulfuric acid wastes deposited in a leaking landfill; an example of transnational externalities would be acid rain in Canada due to U.S. industrial production; an example of global externalities would be the release of ozone-depleting chemicals from refrigerants using CFCs, which destroy atmospheric ozone affecting the penetration of ultraviolet light throughout the world.

When externalities occur locally, they are within the reach of domestic regulation and can be corrected (or "internalized") within national jurisdictions. Taxes, subsidies, and regulation to confront a problem such as a leaking landfill are difficult to devise and enforce even at this level, as evidenced by the experience of the U.S. Superfund, designed to clean up toxic dump sites. But when externalities are transnational, matters of jurisdiction and sovereignty join these issues. In the case of acid rain in Canada caused by U.S. emissions of sulfur dioxide, negotiations at the highest levels of government have been necessary to reach a bilateral agreement on a proper response. NAFTA, the EU, and the tuna-dolphin and U.S.–Canada fisheries cases, considered below, all involve transnational externalities. At the global level, externalities such as atmospheric ozone depletion pose even higher transactions costs if agreements and regulations are to take effect and be enforced.

In short, it is far easier to recommend that environmental externalities be "internalized" than it is to implement and enforce internalization, and implementation and enforcement costs rise as one moves from local to transnational to global cases. Part of the reason for this difficulty is that individuals within nations, as well as governments, vary greatly in their attitudes toward the costs of environmental degradation, and in their willingness to trade off economic benefits for a cleaner and safer environment. This variation is most marked between developed and developing countries. Many developing countries assert with historical justification that the North paid little heed to the environmental consequences in its nineteenth- and twentieth-century rush to industrialization. Only now, as this process proceeds in developing economies, do governments in the North demand that environmental externalities be internalized, at some cost to the pace of economic activity in the South. This is one way in which environmental claims are perceived in the South as a disguised way of protecting home markets in the North.

A major theme at the 1992 Rio Conference was who should pay these costs. Specifically, many developing countries argued that the North should bear a much larger share than reflected in aid flows to date, perhaps by creating a special fund for the purpose. The reaction of many in the North was that this amounted to a form of extortion. The result was that despite many claims of good intentions, few actual commitments were made at Rio. As we will discuss in chapter 6, an alternative would be to join the objectives of the developing countries in GATT (which revolve around greater access to markets in the North) with the environmental objectives of the Rio Conference, offering access to markets in lieu of direct aid.

By granting market access to the South, the North could aid the developing countries far more significantly than through more money for development assistance, which is scarce in any event, in light of budget shortfalls in most of the industrialized economies. At the same time, such market access could be tied to specific attention in the South to environmental protection and improvements, a kind of "environmental conditionality." While developing countries often resent "conditionality" (as when the International Monetary Fund demands anti-inflationary policies in return for loans), it may be a necessary prod in promoting them to raise environmental standards. In many respects, the environmental side agreement to NAFTA provides the clearest constructive example of the benefits of tying market access to a joint commitment to raise environmental standards. Presumably, these environmental improvements can be paid for in part out of the economic benefits of market access.

Despite the possibilities for such linkage, most developing countries have limited scope for major investments in environmental protection comparable to those undertaken in recent years in the North. Whether or not individuals and countries have a preference for an improved environment, the financial wherewithal and political will may simply be lacking, making harmonization of environmental measures a distant goal.[34]

The institutional barriers to dealing effectively with transnational and global externalities are also high. No mechanism exists to set international regulatory or quasi-market incentives comparable to national policies like taxes and subsidies. GATT is clearly not an environmental enforcement agency, and in many respects it is prepared only to deal with issues of trade and the trade effects of environmental policies, rather than to evaluate the merits and demerits of environmental policies themselves, or the environmental impacts of trade flows. The UN Environment Programme (UNEP) also has no capacity to enforce international environmental standards. These institutional issues will be discussed in detail in chapter 6.

At a more technical level, estimating the magnitude of environmental damages and expressing them in dollar terms is not easy. Since the market generally undervalues the environment to begin with, we know that they are larger than they are given credit for; but how large, and thus how to set regulations, taxes, or subsidies, is a difficult problem of estimation. In many respects, environmental judgments take on a moral dimension, often involving future generations, which is inherently difficult to reduce to economic terms. Even in economic analysis, environmental benefits like clean air are "public goods" (and environmental damages such as water pollution "public bads"), so they are difficult to attribute directly to a beneficiary. Many individuals thus do not pay for them, acting as free riders, and it is difficult, except hypothetically, to say how much they *would* pay. This confounds efforts to set regulatory or tax/ subsidy schemes.

Despite these difficulties, economists are increasingly active in trying to find mechanisms to confront environmental damages, which represent a major category of social loss. In addition to losses in economic efficiency (such as a failure to consume petroleum fuels in ways that burn them efficiently, reducing smog and air pollution), environmental degradation causes more tangible human losses.[35] These include health effects leading to disease and premature death from water and air pollution, injuries from improper handling of hazardous wastes, and increased levels of infant mortality. Such losses in human welfare can be compared to the displacement of workers, whose involuntary unemployment is also a form of social waste. When these losses accompany trade liberalization, a dilemma is created for its advocates unless adverse impacts on the environment and on workers are squarely and jointly addressed.

Targets and Instruments

A commitment to joint consideration of trade and environmental objectives does not suggest that they be merged, or that trade-offs may not be necessary. A principle of economic planning developed by economist Jan Tinbergen, the Nobel laureate, is that in general each target of policy merits a separate instrument aimed at it. Environmental targets, in other words, are generally best met by environmental policies; trade targets by trade policies. Whereas environmental problems may be *reinforced* by trade policies, they are unlikely to be best resolved though trade measures alone. Instead, some *combination* of trade and environmental policies will be most efficient.[36] In fact, the advantages of trade policy reform can be lost if appropriate environmental actions are not undertaken jointly (see appendix A). Put the other way around, environmental and trade policy reforms are often complementary and mutually *reinforcing*.[37]

The interdependence of trade and environment has gained the attention of both the environmental and the trade communities in large measure because critics contend that trade liberalization is likely to exacerbate environmental problems. However, if this interdependence is acknowledged, and appropriately targeted environmental interventions accompany trade policy reform, such fears are less warranted. Indeed, if an appropriately balanced combination of environmental and trade policy measures is found, the result can be welfare gains both from trade reforms *and* from improvements in the level of environmental quality.

The analysis of environmental and trade targets and instruments suggests four principles of balanced trade and environmental policies. Together, these principles can serve as a focus of discussion and, one hopes, as a basis for reform. The first principle simply restates the logic of matching targets and instruments. The second two consider trade and environmental policies, respectively, and how the domain of each might reasonably be determined in practice. The fourth principle extends this logic to the multilateral setting.

Principle 1: In general, trade targets should be matched with trade instruments, and environmental targets with environmental instruments. This principle is not inviolate, and some "cross-matching" may be justified for some cases. A trade measure mismatched by being directed at environmental problems is the subject of a GATT and U.S.–Canada panel ruling, discussed in chapter 4, that Canadian landing restrictions on U.S. salmon and herring fishing boats were not primarily aimed at environmental targets, but in fact acted as trade restrictions.

Principle 2: In general, trade policies should aim to reduce trade barriers while remaining environmentally neutral. If these policies nonetheless create (or fail to reduce) adverse environmental damages, then the problem requires a separate environmental intervention.

Principle 3: In general, environmental policies should aim to conserve natural resources and improve the quality of the ecosystem while remaining trade-neutral. If these policies nonetheless create trade distortions, then the problem requires a separate trade policy intervention.

Together, principles 2 and 3 suggest that trade and environment be separate spheres of policy, but that policymakers in each sphere keep an eye on the other, since they are bound to overlap in some cases. In the discussion over NAFTA, U.S. vegetable growers contended that U.S. restrictions on pesticide use put them at a competitive disadvantage vis-à-vis Mexican growers, who are subject to more lax restrictions. Rather than reducing the level of U.S. environmental regulation, an appropriate response to this trade issue would be to negotiate, bilaterally or multilaterally, equivalent standards in the Mexican case, or to demonstrate that the Mexican standards justify an import restriction. This is the general route the environmental side agreement to NAFTA follows.

Principle 4: National governments should be encouraged to pursue similar trade and environmental policy objectives. When applied at the multilateral level, the logic of targets and instruments suggests the need to coordinate not only trade but also environmental policies across national borders. This will result in less distorted trade and a more readily protected global environment. Thus, multilateral organizations, such as GATT, and regional trading arrangements, such as NAFTA and the EU, should seek to promote consensus over the general objectives of both trade and environmental policy. This is not to argue that different countries should seek exactly "the same" standards or policies. However, because of the growing number of recognizably transnational and global externalities, national trade *and* environmental policies require greater coordination across national borders. This coordination is not a substitute for national policies, nor does agreement on objectives (for example, CFC emissions) imply that the same actions to achieve them should be undertaken in different countries.[38] Indeed, major questions, assuming agreement on objectives can be reached, are how to allow for national diversity in meeting these objectives, and what new institutions should address themselves to the challenge.

AN ENVIRONMENTAL PERSPECTIVE

The legal and economic perspectives we have considered have hinted at but not squarely addressed an underlying issue: that the international trading system and national economic policies have failed to give sufficient priority to the environment. If a true balance between trade and the environment is to be achieved, the trading system and the national and international institutions that undergird it must accept changes. These changes will result in far more explicit recognition of the need for reduced environmental damages, and a search for complementarity between trade and environmental policies. This is not to suggest simply that trade must give way to demands from environmental interests, but rather that we integrate environmental concerns, giving them a priority equal to arguments for trade reforms. This balanced approach would create a synthesis of legal, economic, and environmental perspectives, based in three common observations.

The first is closely related to the targets and instruments discussion above. While it derives from economic policy, it has direct implications for both trade and environmental rule making. The power of the targets and instruments distinction is to emphasize that in the many cases where trade and environment remain separate spheres, little will be gained from using trade instruments as a response to environmental problems, or vice versa. If a trade measure has no obvious environmental consequences, then scarce resources can be better used in improving the trade policy than in conducting an environmental impact assessment. Eliminating textile quotas, for example, would be beneficial to the trading system in its own right, and would have only remote implications for environmental quality. Likewise, when responding to national environmental problems imposes no additional burdens on trade, it is best to employ the most effective environmental interventions available. Establishing an effective environmental basis for cleaning up landfills in the United States should not require the involvement of trade policymakers.

The issues of primary concern in this volume, of course, are those in which trade and environmental spheres collide, and where the choice of appropriate instruments is therefore complicated. The second observation is that in these cases, a logical sequence of resolution is still possible, in which costs and benefits are estimated on both the trade and the environmental sides of the ledger. Where trade measures lead to environmental damages, these damages, once documented, require enforced regulations. From an economic perspective, an "externality" has resulted from the failure of the market to account for the environmental effects of trade. Enforced regulation should be understood to include quasi-market instruments such as taxes, fees, or subsidies. The principles of matching targets and instruments *still* imply that the damages are best addressed by an environmental regulatory response, rather than a trade instrument. However, the impact of the externality may be transnational, or global, implying very different types of responses. Especially in cases of transnational or global damages, some of these responses will inevitably impinge on trade.

If an environmental measure leads to trade burdens, then the question is whether these burdens are justified under several alternative but essentially similar criteria. All of these legal criteria, interestingly, involve a similar judgment: whether the benefits of the environmental measure (estimated or assumed) exceed the costs to the parties in the form of lost or diverted trade. Naturally, disagreement between the parties over these questions is to be expected, and not all elements of this judgment are strictly quantifiable. In particular, where international trade and environmental agreements create obviously conflicting or ambiguous obligations, some form of temporary waiver may be necessary so that issues of priority and consistency can receive international attention over time.

The third observation is that the institutional level at which resolution of disputes occurs will be a critical question for policymakers. In cases of trade-induced environmental damage, or environmental measures that impose trade burdens, or conflicts between trade and environmental rules or treaties, policymakers will need to consider the institutional capacity to respond at the local (national or subnational) level, the transnational (bilateral) level, or the global (multilateral) level. Each level of intervention poses different problems and advantages. If expanded trade with Mexico will aggravate environmental problems, then both the

United States and Mexico will need to devote internal regulatory resources to confronting the problems created. Yet actions taken by each nation (and states within the nations) will function more effectively if they are coordinated. This is the proposed function of the new institutions created during the NAFTA side agreement process. Such institutions are critical where the externalities involved are transnational or global.

Some trade-environment disputes cannot be resolved through national institutions or bilateral understandings, while some might be better resolved in this way than multilaterally. One of the greatest global institutional challenges will be to design multilateral *environmental* institutions with the capacity to oversee international environmental agreements, and to relate them to the trade measures proposed and enforced under GATT. This institutional expression of the balance between trade and the environment will be developed in chapter 6. Before considering this institutional reform, it may be useful to look at a variety of cases that illustrate the issues discussed thus far.

Chapter 3

Trade Agreements and the Environment: The EU and NAFTA

Will trade liberalization lead to increased damage to the environment? This chapter considers this question at several levels. At one level, these environmental damages derive from the "scale effects" of freer trade, resulting from increases in the quantity of goods and services moving within countries and across borders. In the case of the EU or NAFTA, greater economic integration may lead to greater transportation needs, higher levels of manufacturing output, and general increases in the demand for raw and processed products, all of which impose greater wear and tear on natural ecosystems. A particularly striking example of these impacts is the pollution found in the rapidly growing Mexican-U.S. border region. Differences in environmental standards, especially between developed economies in the North and developing economies of the South, may also create "pollution havens" for firms and industries seeking less regulatory oversight. Finally, the proposed harmonization of environmental standards is argued to lead to a "lowest common denominator," in which higher levels of environmental protection are sacrificed in the name of competitiveness. Yet protection is also an environmental culprit, as the EU and NAFTA experience make clear.

EU INTERNAL MARKET

The EU provides important lessons in the primary issues of trade and environment. First, its experience with growth through internal trade liberalization offers insights into the extent to which this process results in environmental damages, and the ways in which EU regulations have responded. Second, it provides examples of environmental measures that may cause burdens to internal EU trade, as well as examples of protectionist trade policies (especially vis-à-vis the rest of the world) with adverse environmental implications. Despite a mixed record on both trade and the environment (in a world where no government is free of guilt), the EU has achieved a level of integration of both areas that merits careful attention. Its experience offers evidence to support the possibility of balancing the forces of trade integration and environmental protection.

No chapter of this length can give full consideration to the complexity and detail of European environmental and trade policy; the focus here will be somewhat narrowly based on several illustrative examples. After brief consideration of the EU and its history in the environmental policy area, we focus on the environmental consequences of trade integration, and the possible environmental consequences of trade diversion, due to protection of various EU sectors, notably agriculture and transport. Finally, we consider the attempt to balance trade and environmental interests in the EU, and offer some tentative conclusions.

The EU is the creation of the 1957 Treaty of Rome,[1] and now comprises twelve member states: Belgium, Denmark, France, Germany, Great Britain, Greece, Ireland, Italy, Luxembourg, the Netherlands, Portugal, and Spain. Its purpose is to promote the free transfer of goods, capital, and services. As part of completing the internal process of integration, the EU has addressed the linkages between trade and environment directly, and has been active in setting environmental policies and resolving trade-environment disputes.[2] In assessing its experience and the lessons it can provide, one must keep in mind some of its institutional characteristics.

Several institutional features of the EU are relevant to this discussion.[3] First, the EU is a supranational institution, and member

countries have surrendered at least some of their national sovereignty to the European Commission. The Commission has a full
directorate general (DG XII) with responsibility for environmental
policy, civil protection, and nuclear safety. Second, the EU controls
funds (approximately 1.2 billion European Currency Units [ECU],
equal to $1.4 billion in 1993) that can be allocated to helping its
members in upgrading their environmental performance. This provides it with more authority and a wider range of instruments than
many other international institutions have in dealing with member
countries' environmental policies. Third, the proximity of member
countries, the free flow of labor, and the high level of intra-EU trade
strengthens the case for greater harmonization, and makes problems of transnational pollution more obvious, demanding higher
levels of political attention.

The EU's Single European Act of 1987, together with the
Maastricht Treaty, provides rather specific prescriptions for environmental standard setting, including a policy of upward harmonization for health, safety, and environmental regulations (and a
general EU objective of environmental protection based on preventive action, reduction of damages at their source, and the "polluter-
pays principle"). The Single European Act amended the Treaty of
Rome to provide a mandate for harmonization, while adding specific safeguards concerning health, safety, and environment protection to "take as a base of a high level of protection." It thus allows
members to adopt standards that are more stringent than other
members', provided they are not protectionist.[4] The EU also provides for the "subsidiarity principle," which means that intervention should occur at the lowest level of authority with competence to
manage a given problem. This implies that member states should be
relatively free to establish their own product standards, subject to
the constraints implied by EU "directives." Such directives, defined
in article 198 of the European Economic Community Treaty, may
also require unanimity by the EU members (depending on the treaty
basis cited for action) and are therefore subject to a "watering
down" process.[5]

The subsidiarity principle is balanced by the doctrine of mutual
recognition, reinforced in 1978 by the European Court of Justice, in
its famous *Cassis de Dijon* decision, which ruled against a German

law requiring beverages defined as "liqueurs" to have a minimum alcohol content of 25 percent. This law had prevented sales in Germany of Cassis de Dijon, a French black-currant liqueur with an alcohol content of 15.26 percent. The Court could find no public health justification for the law, and struck it down, arguing in favor of the doctrine of mutual recognition. Specifically, the Court stated that member states were free to maintain their own standards on products produced and sold within their territory (here Germany), but could not prevent the domestic sale of products meeting the standards of other states (here France) unless they were necessary to protect public health or the consumer from harm. In effect, to use the language of chapter 2, the Court could find no justification for the burden on trade imposed by the German law. In further elaboration, the European Court found in a separate matter that even if an imported product contained additives that were illegal in the importing state—specifically, additives to beer that violated Germany purity standards (*Reinheitsgebot*)—the product could not be barred unless shown to be dangerous, in which case the response should be "proportional" to the danger.[6]

In the 1980s two additional cases reinforced the power of the EU and its primary regulatory authority, the European Commission, to legislate on the environment. In 1980, in *Commission v. Italy*, the Commission brought an enforcement action against Italy's failure to implement a Commission directive on the sulfur content of liquid fuels. In 1985, in *Procureur de la République v. Association de Défense des Bruleurs d'Huiles Usagées*, the Commission interpreted measures to restrict trade activities (in this case activities of a prosecutor against a trade association of waste oil–burning manufacturers and stove users) as follows:

> . . . in so far as such measures . . . have a restrictive effect on the freedom of trade and of competition, they must nevertheless neither be discriminatory nor go beyond the inevitable restrictions which are justified by the pursuit of the objective of environmental protection, which is in the general interest.[7]

The environmental provisions of the Single European Act and subsequent actions responded to these cases, although tension continues between the desire of member states for more scope and the desire of the European Commission for an upper regulatory hand.

Overall, these efforts to confront trade-environment conflicts allow the member states considerable latitude under "subsidiarity" to set higher environmental standards so long as they are justified. However, especially in the consumer and food safety case, they have also led to complaints of disguised protectionism as between member states.[8] Similar fears exist in the rest of the world, especially in the United States. In March 1991 the EU announced a two-stage program aimed at harmonizing antipollution measures corresponding to the highest level "reasonably envisaged in light of the latest scientific and technological findings." According to some sources, this has raised concerns over whether such measures will be used as barriers to market access.[9]

Environmental Impacts of Market Integration in the EU

Because of the close quarters of the EU, concern over possible environmental damages due to unregulated growth promoted by integration led the European Commission to convene a task force in 1988 to study the environmental impacts of the realization of the internal market.[10] While the task force was a small element of EU action in the context of the Single European Act and the 1992 integration process, it provided a valuable appraisal and typology of different impacts of integration on the environment. First, it delineated three types of possible impacts: static effects, spatial effects, and dynamic effects.

Static effects result from the removal of border checks caused by the harmonization of technical standards and regulations, the reduction of market entry barriers, and the opening up of public procurement. Since border checks are used to control the movement of nuclear and hazardous waste and to meet obligations under international treaties relating to trade in rare and endangered species, their removal might pose problems of enforcement. Similarly, technical standards and regulations are used to ensure that products are environmentally acceptable, and harmonization must therefore maintain these protections. To the extent that border controls are removed or modified, and no alternative policy measures are put in place, a number of factors may cause environmental damage: large-scale tourism, the circulation of products originating in countries without stringent product controls, market entry leading to increased road haulage and air transportation, and fewer land use controls. These concerns are remarkably similar to many expressed in North America over NAFTA.

Spatial effects relate to changes in the geographic distribution of economic activity, such as transportation and tourism. For example, expected growth in the transportation sector and especially in road and plane traffic will affect environmental conditions along transitways and in the vicinity of airports. Increased access may lead to increases in development of coastal areas and mountain regions.

Dynamic effects relate to changes resulting from increased competition—namely, increased economic growth; more efficient use of capital, labor, and land; and more rapid technological progress. The main impacts on the environment may occur through increases in energy use, transport-sector activity, and domestic and commercial waste, and through changes in land uses.

The EU study noted that all of these effects may lead to environmental damages in one of three ways. First, damages may occur because of the sheer increase in quantities of goods and services traded, which are accompanied by pollution, similar to the scale effects discussed earlier. Second, as industrial structure changes in response to integration, pollution-intensive industries may either grow in importance or find alternative venues inside or outside the EU. Finally, as environmental regulatory oversight changes in the EU, and older technologies become outmoded, new technologies emerge in all sectors, including pollution control. Ultimately, the impacts of trade integration on the environment are determined by the complex interaction between static, spatial, and dynamic effects, and by the volume of trade, industrial structure, and technologies in use.

The Agricultural Sector

These distinctions are useful in generally appraising and categorizing the environmental impacts of trade integration, but the ultimate basis of such appraisal must be individual examples. One of the most striking (and politically sensitive) examples of the impacts of such integration on the environment is the Common Agricultural Policy (CAP) of the EU. The integration of the agricultural sector is only one type of trade integration occurring within the EU, but it is perhaps the most "mature" case of integrated trade, and agriculture is often cited as the most truly "common" of the EU market sectors. One cost of this internal achievement has been that the EU's agricultural relationship with the rest of the world is one of protectionism and trade diversion. Through a complex scheme of subsidies paid to farmers, Europe has created incentives for chronic internal overproduction by protecting its internal market from global competition through border taxes that restrict market access. EU farmers' domestic prices are protected at the border by levies charged on incoming commodities, while surpluses are discharged from the Community through export subsidies ("restitutions") that pay down the difference between internal and external prices. Despite efforts since 1988 to discipline this system by setting production ceilings and reducing supported price levels, and by designing land set-asides to reduce crop production, the agricultural portion of the EU budget continues to demand as much as half of total budgetary resources, and chronic surpluses remain a problem.

The history and functioning of the CAP are beyond the scope of this chapter, but it is important to emphasize that its original objectives revolved around trade policy and food security, and that environmental considerations were clearly secondary. It is even possible to argue, as does Konrad von Moltke, that the sins of the CAP should not be laid at the feet of the EU integration.[11] Over time, however, the intensification and specialization of European agriculture in response to large subsidies and protectionist border measures has aroused alarm in environmental circles. The Food and Agriculture Organization (FAO) of the UN, in its Seventeenth Regional Conference for Europe, identified four major environmental problems resulting directly from intensive European agricultural production.[12] These are as follows:

- Pollution and contamination of soil, water, air, and food resulting from increased agrichemical use and livestock effluents

- Degradation of natural resources and, particularly, deterioration in the quality of soil, water, forest, and traditional rural landscapes

- Disturbance and reduction of biotopes and wildlife habitats

- Reduction in wildlife species and loss of biological and genetic diversity

Table 1 summarizes the effects of these problems. Among the specific examples the FAO cited were soil contamination and air pollution from ammonia in animal wastes due to concentrated cattle and hog facilities that have responded to subsidies in the livestock and feed sector.

Utilizing the Commission's task force distinctions, one can argue that while the CAP has removed some static barriers to internal agricultural trade, its primary impacts have been to reorient the spatial concentration of agricultural production and to generate dynamic competitive and technological changes. These have included the relocation of grain and oilseed production, as well as livestock, to a far greater extent than was true in the pre-CAP period, when European agriculture involved many more diversified farms. By supporting farm prices above world market levels, the CAP has induced the intensive rearing of livestock and heavy applications of farm chemicals, leading to the soil and water pollution problems cited by the FAO. European agricultural economists Monika Hartmann and Alan Matthews report that nitrogen fertilizer use in the EU is more than three times that in the United States, and pesticide use per unit of land area is over twice as great. In the Netherlands, pesticide use is more than ten times that of the United States.[13] Livestock stocking rates and the concentration of facilities have led to a situation in which 15 percent of all dairy cows and 25 percent of all pigs are concentrated on less than 4 percent of all agricultural land.[14]

Given the levels of environmental concern generated by EU agricultural policy, it is tempting to conclude that integration itself is responsible for the damages. However, the primary mechanism of integration *within* the EU agriculture sector has been price supports, which turn on border measures imposed on those *outside* the Community. By insulating EU agriculture from the rest of the world, it is the protectionist element of the CAP, more than its effect on internal integration, that has contributed to environmental degradation by subsidizing and protecting concentrated agricultural production using techniques that are environmentally hazardous and that have only recently come under regulatory oversight.

TABLE 1.   ENVIRONMENTAL EFFECTS OF INTENSIVE AGRICULTURAL
PRACTICES IN THE EU

Pollution and contamination

Practice	Soil	Water	Air	Food	Soil quality
Drainage of wetlands, land reclamation	Accelerated pollution due to loss of "ecosystem services"	Accelerated pollution due to loss of "ecosystem services"			Soil dehydration, degradation
Conversion of pastures, forests, etc.					Reduction in nutrients; changes in soil hydrology; erosion
Consolidation of fields, removal of hedges, walls, etc.					Inadequate management, leading to degradation
Tillage, use of heavy machinery			Combustion gases		Compaction of soil; wind and water erosion; reduced productivity
Application of synthetic fertilizers	Nitrogen saturation; concentration of heavy metals	Nitrates, heavy metals, leached into surface and groundwater	Evaporation	Nitrate contamination of food crops, shellfish	Reduced fertility; accumulation of heavy metals

TABLE 1 (*continued*)

Natural resource degradation			Biotope and habitat disturbance	Loss of wildlife and genetic diversity
Water/aquatic resources	Forest resources	Landscape amenities		
Changes in ground water table, water cycles		Loss of natural areas valued for conservation	Negative effects on water-related ecosystems; loss of terrestrial and aquatic habitats	Loss or extinction of flora and fauna species, particularly fish and waterfowl
Flooding, siltation, sedimentation of water systems	Loss of forest vegetation, ground cover; loss of pasture for game, domestic animals	Decrease in recreational amenities; loss of heritage values; degradation of rural landscapes	Loss of complex biotopes of special ecological value, e.g., natural forests; destruction of habitats	Loss or extinction of species; diminished variety of wildlife; loss of genetic resources
Negative effects on water conservation and management		As above	Reduction in number and complexity of habitats maintained by the traditional agricultural ecosystems	Loss of species abundance and diversity, particularly birds and insects
Heavy silting, sedimentation of water systems		Landscape degradation	Disturbance of soil ecosystems	Adverse effects on soil organisms, microflora, and microfauna
Eutrophication; contamination of aquifers	Loss of alluvial forests	Loss of recreational amenities	Destruction of biotopes and loss of terrestrial and aquatic habitats due to pollution, contamination, and eutrophication	Loss or extinction of wide range of species; diminished diversity of plant and animal life; adverse effects on soil organisms, etc.; loss of genetic resources

TABLE 1 (*continued*)

Pollution and contamination

Practice	Soil	Water	Air	Food	Soil quality
Spreading of manure, slurry	Nitrogen saturation; concentration of phosphates, heavy metals	Nitrates, phosphates, heavy metals leached into surface and groundwaters	Release of ammonia, leading to acidification	Nitrate contamination of food crops, shellfish	Reduced fertility; acidification; structural damage
Application of pesticides	Residues, degradation products	Residues, etc. leached into surface and groundwaters	Evaporation; spray drift	Residues in food crops, livestock	Accumulation of residues
Irrigation	Excess salts	Salinization; accelerated pollution			Salinization; water logging; erosion
Straw burning			Local pollution		
Abandonment of marginal lands					Erosion; rural desertification

Sources: Food and Agriculture Organization (FAO), Policy Analysis Division, *Socioeconomic Aspects of Environmental Policies in European Agriculture.* (Prepared for the Seventeenth Regional Conference for Europe, Venice, February, 1990); and information provided by FAO, OECD, ISEP and CEC.

TABLE 1 *(continued)*

Natural resource degradation			Biotope and habitat disturbance	Loss of wildlife and genetic diversity
Water/aquatic resources	Forest resources	Landscape amenities		
Eutrophication; contamination of aquifers	Damage from acidification	Loss of recreational amenities, aesthetic values	As above	As above
Contamination of aquifers	Loss of alluvial forests	Loss of recreational amenities	As above	Loss or extinction of non-target flora and fauna, particularly fish, birds, and insects; buildup of resistance in plants and insects
Saline contamination of aquifers; reduction in groundwater levels		Landscape degradation	Negative effects on aquatic ecosystems, habitats	Loss or extinction of species; reduction in ecological diversity
		Reduction in local landscape amenities and aesthetic values	Disturbance of biotopes, habitats; risk of destruction by spreading fire	Reduction in species
Silting, sedimentation of surface waters		Landscape degradation	Loss of activity supporting biotopes; decline in number and complexity of habitats	Reduction in species

The relatively inexpensive animal fodder offered by Thailand to the Netherlands, where the majority of manioc is shipped into the Port of Rotterdam, has contributed (together with the overriding influence of EU price subsidies) to adverse environmental impacts, both in the EU and in Thailand. As noted above, the intensive pig industry in the Netherlands is a major source of nitrate pollution, leading to contamination of existing water sources and huge demands for additional water, which have encouraged underground infiltration of saline water from the oceans.[20] In northeastern Thailand, manioc growing takes place in the dry Dipterocarpus forests, where land is cleared to support the profitable export market. The forest has shrunk 60 percent since 1950, with deforestation attributable to expanded manioc production. The result has been major soil erosion problems. Manioc is a highly erosive crop, and rapidly draws fertility down on already depleted soils.[21] As in the case of the CAP, ending protectionist agreements such as the one with Thailand would have the additional effect of broadening the sources of starch imports to the EU. Its impacts on environmental damages would, of course, also depend on reductions in incentives for intensive pig production in the EU.

Even so, it is clear that in the EU, as elsewhere, trade liberalization alone cannot mitigate problems of agricultural pollution. Additional enforcement of environmental regulations is necessary. In 1987 a modest program of financial aid to encourage farmers to engage in environmental protection in "sensitive areas" was introduced, and subsequent financial support has been made available under "structural policy" programs in a number of states for farmers willing to invest in pollution control technologies. However, only 3 percent of the total EU budget is spent on structural policy, while around 60 percent continues to be devoted to agricultural price supports.[22]

In addition to the "sensitive areas" program, the EU has used a land set-aside program since 1988 in attempts to control agricultural surpluses. Member states are given considerable latitude in determining which lands to retire from agricultural production. The environmental impact, according to Hartmann and Matthews, has been "relatively marginal," since participation is thus far voluntary. As of 1990–1991, only about 2 percent of the EU's total arable land was enrolled, and evidence indicates that the land remaining in production will be even more intensively framed "through the substitution of agricultural chemicals for the now-even-scarcer land."[23] When land set-aside is left uncared for, it can also lead to increased erosion and water pollution.

In 1991 the EU announced a stricter regulatory response to agriculture in the form of a "nitrate directive," requiring member states to designate "vulnerable zones" where a "code of good agricultural practice" must be introduced. The consequences of the directive are still unclear, and many details have yet to be implemented, although some analysts believe that it will contribute to marginally reduced livestock production.[24] When and if the nitrate directive is accompanied by substantial general reductions in price support, exports of surplus EU production could fall substantially, although most of the effect appears likely to result directly from price support reductions and only indirectly from the nitrate directive. The directive itself is estimated to reduce nitrogen fertilizer consumption at the margin, depending on whether it is accompanied by price support reductions.[25]

The Transport Sector

As in the agricultural sector, the linkages from trade to environment in the EU transport sector are complex. Even so, it is in the transport sector that the European Commission's task force expects some of the greatest environmental impacts from integration.[26] Table 3 shows some of these effects.

Integration is likely to alter the number of transport vehicles in the air and on rail. The spatial distribution of newer versus older and more polluting modes of transport will likely shift as northern Europe implements stricter pollution control technologies than the Mediterranean economies in the south. Significant increases in passenger traffic and road freight movements are expected, especially along heavily used corridors such as the east-west link from Venice to Milan in northern Italy, where climatic factors at the base of the Alps create thermal inversions and intense levels of air pollution. Removal of border controls is expected to increase the number of long-distance hauls, thus aggravating such conditions. Liberal-

TABLE 3.   ENVIRONMENTAL EFFECTS OF PRINCIPAL TRANSPORT MODES IN THE EU

Transport mode	Raw material use	Air	Water resources	Land resources	Solid waste	Noise	Risk of accident	Other impacts
Road	Mineral oils	Air pollution (Carbon monoxide, hydrocarbons, and nitrous oxides; particulates and fuel additives such as lead)	Pollution of surface water and groundwater by surface runoff; modification of water systems by road building	Land taken for infrastructures; extraction of road-building materials	Abandoned spoil tips and rubble from road works, road vehicles withdrawn from service; waste oil	Noise and vibration from cars, motorcycles, and trucks in cities and along main roads	Deaths, injuries, and property damaged from road accidents; risk of transport of hazardous substances; risk of structural failure in old or worn road facilities	Partition or destruction of neighborhoods, farmland, and habitats; congestion

		Air pollution						
Air	Kerosene	Air pollution	Modification of water tables, river courses, and field drainage in airport construction	Land taken for infrastructures; dereliction of obsolete facilities	Aircraft withdrawn from service	Noise around airports	Aircraft accidents	
Marine and inland water	Mineral oils		Modification of water systems during port construction and canal cutting and dredging	Land taken for infrastructures; dereliction of port facilities and canals	Vessels and craft withdrawn from service		Bulk transport of fuels and hazardous substances	
Rail	Coal, oil for electricity			Land taken for rights of way and terminals; dereliction of obsolete facilities	Abandoned lines, equipment, and rolling stock	Noise and vibration around terminals and along railways	Derailment or collision of freight carrying hazardous substances	Partition or destruction of neighborhoods, farmland, and wildlife habitats

Source: Task Force on Environment and the Internal Market, 1992: *The Environmental Dimension* (Bonn: Economica, Verlag, 1990), p. 102.

ization of air travel and increasing demands for rapid movement of freight and air passengers will aggravate already crowded conditions, unless rapid rail transport can relieve some of this pressure.

In contrast with the environmental impacts on the agricultural sector, those on the European transport sector derive largely from the integration and liberalization of internal trade, rather than from protectionist policies vis-à-vis the rest of the world. It is thus clear that no unique or simple link connects liberalization or protection to negative environmental effects. In both sectors, the burdens imposed on the environment are likely to require new regulations enforced both at the Community level and at the level of the member states in order to respond to these negative effects.

Lessons for Policy

It is unclear whether the current institutional capacity in the EU Commission is sufficient to the task of Community-wide environmental regulation. Strong leadership at the Community level is needed to avoid multiple, competing national solutions to similar environmental problems. Also unclear is whether management by "directives," given the high levels of independence granted to member states under the subsidiarity principle, will allow national and EU-wide environmental interventions to succeed. Nonetheless, subsidiarity has been critical to the political argument in favor of the Maastricht Treaty, since it has reduced the force of claims that Maastricht will undermine national environmental initiatives. These arguments closely parallel those in opposition to NAFTA and GATT, in which sovereignty is said to be threatened. Even so, the EU's supranational environmental institutions provide important insights into the need, at a more global level, for institutional capacity responsive to the environmental consequences of trade measures, whether these measures are protectionist or liberalizing.

The first insight from the EU experience is that some degree of subsidiarity will be required, if only because environmental policy remains largely in the domain of national governments. Second, this principle must be balanced by overarching institutional capacity to deny states the right to impose burdens on trade, *and* to protect the environment from negative trade impacts. Third, the capacity for intervention affecting both trade and the environment must carry the legitimacy accorded in the EU to the European Commission and the European Court of Justice. Fourth, substantial budgetary resources will be needed to enforce environmental regulations over time. Each of these issues recurred, in different forms, in the debate over NAFTA.

NAFTA

NAFTA is a precedent-setting agreement that opens markets between two developed countries (the United States and Canada) and a developing country (Mexico),while retaining a variety of environmental and labor safeguards through "side agreements." NAFTA was a lightning rod for political opponents of trade reform, especially among some environmentalists. Although NAFTA poses some of the same issues of market integration as the EU has faced (especially during the accession of Spain, Portugal, and Greece), the even larger gap in enforced regulatory standards between Mexico on the one hand and the United States and Canada on the other has made NAFTA more controversial.

One of the central criticisms of NAFTA has been the impact of expanded trade on the environment. The prominence of the issue is due in part to the major environmental problems experienced in the border region pre-NAFTA, where the *maquiladora* sector[27] became the focus of widespread criticism because of the absence of enforced environmental regulations. Many members of the environmental community feel that unless NAFTA is accompanied by enforced environmental safeguards, it will lead to additional environmental damages. Because such damages will cross the borders of the agreement's signatories, the appropriate regulatory response is not only enforced regulations in the home markets of the three nations, but trilateral instruments responsive to the transnational character of the externalities involved. These instruments emerged in August 1993, in the form of an environmental side agreement to NAFTA that created the trilateral Commission on Environmental Cooperation (CEC), with important new, precedent-setting powers of oversight and enforcement. Even so, some environmental opponents of NAFTA remained opposed to the total agreement, which narrowly passed the House of Representatives in November 1993. Senate passage followed quickly, and NAFTA was signed by President Clinton on December 8, 1993.

Despite similar U.S. and Canadian concerns over environmental issues, the majority of criticism of NAFTA has focused on the wide gaps in enforced regulations between the United States and Mexico. In response to this criticism, the Bush administration and the Mexican government included provisions in NAFTA—even before the Clinton side agreements—designed to encourage higher Mexican environmental standards and compliance. Former U.S. Trade Representative Carla Hills stated in 1992 that NAFTA went "further than any previous trade agreement in addressing environmental concerns and actively promoting environmental protection."[28] Environmentalists' calls for more and stricter environmental regulations as part of a final NAFTA package led to the negotiation of the side agreement in 1993, which was incorporated into the final NAFTA deal.

Three main issues emerged from the debate over NAFTA. Most generally, what implications will NAFTA actually have for the environment in North America? Second, how can the environmental protections attached to NAFTA through side agreements be made to work? Third, when environmental and trade objectives under NAFTA come into conflict, what principles should guide decisions over them, and how will the CEC make these decisions? The discussion of these questions begins with a general description of NAFTA, its participants, and expected economic impacts. Next, NAFTA's implications for the environment are examined, including the *maquiladora* industries and the potential for pollution havens. Finally, the challenges faced by the environmental side agreement are discussed, particularly, whether it can develop the institutional authority to regulate transnational externalities without jettisoning the benefits that more open trade can provide.

What Is NAFTA?

In June of 1990, President George Bush and Mexican President Carlos Salinas de Gortari agreed to begin free trade negotiations; Canada joined the negotiations in early 1991. The objectives of

NAFTA were to "eliminate barriers to trade, promote conditions of fair competition, increase investment opportunities, provide adequate protection for intellectual property rights, establish effective procedures for the implementation and application of the Agreement and for the resolution of disputes and to further trilateral, regional and multilateral cooperation."[29] Although negotiations between the Bush administration and the Mexican and Canadian governments were completed on August 12, 1992, and the document was signed on December 17, 1992, President Clinton promised during the 1992 election campaign that he would not forward a final NAFTA text to Congress without a set of environmental safeguards. Under U.S. law, final approval of the text required that ninety calendar days be set aside for congressional consideration and public hearings, followed by ninety days of congressional session (Congress is typically in session about three days a week) for debate over implementing legislation before a final, up-or-down vote.

In addition to an environmental side agreement, safeguards affecting labor standards and "import surges" were negotiated and announced August 13, 1993. In the weeks and days before the vote in the House of Representatives, numerous other agreements external to the text were made with members of Congress.

Now that it is finally approved, NAFTA will create a market of over 360 million people. Table 4 shows the gross national product (GNP), GNP per capita, population in 1990, and recent growth rates for Canada, Mexico, and the United States. Since the U.S. GNP is 25 times that of Mexico, and 10 times that of Canada, it is clear that the free trade agreement will have considerably larger implications for Mexico and Canada than for the United States. While many sectors would gain in Mexico, some—such as highly traditional and protected agricultural producers—will likely fall in number, much as their counterparts did in Spain, Portugal, and Greece following the accession of these nations to the EU.

NAFTA builds upon the Canadian-U.S. Free Trade Agreement, which came into effect on January 1, 1989, when a plan for U.S.-Canadian tariff elimination over ten years commenced. Prior to the agreement with Canada, the average Canadian tariff on dutiable

TABLE 4. GNP, GNP PER CAPITA, POPULATION, AND GROWTH RATES, 1990.

Country	GNP (billions of $)	Real growth rate (1980–1990)	GNP per capita ($)	Real growth rate (1980–1990)	Population (millions)	Growth rate (%) (1980–1990)
Canada	543	3.3	20,450	2.4	26.5	0.9
Mexico	215	1.1	2,490	−0.9	86.2	2.0
United States	5,446	3.2	21,700	2.2	250.9	1.0
Total	6,204				363.6	

Source: World Bank, *The World Bank Atlas, 1991* (Washington, D.C., 1991), pp. 6–9.

imports from the United States was about 9 percent, while the average U.S. import tariff on dutiable goods from Canada was 3 percent.[30] When weighted by value imported, 1991 Mexican tariffs on imports of U.S. products averaged about 11 percent, and U.S. tariffs on the import of Mexican goods averaged about 4 percent.[31] For all commodities traded between the United States and Mexico, under NAFTA, tariffs for both countries that are not immediately eliminated will be phased out over five or ten years. For some especially sensitive commodities, tariffs will be phased out over fifteen years.[32] Table 5 lists the main commodities traded between Mexico, Canada, and the United States, and the estimated effects of tariff removal and U.S. quota expansion, together with the effective tariff levels.

The results of one analysis of NAFTA, examining two scenarios, are shown in Table 6. In the first scenario, tariffs and nontariff barriers were reduced, but no changes in capital flows were projected. In the second scenario, tariff and nontariff barriers were reduced, and capital flows into Mexico were allowed to reflect changing investment patterns. According to this analysis, increased capital flows into Mexico will account for a large share of the benefits of the free trade agreement. In the increased capital flows scenario, Mexico realizes the largest percentage gain in GDP (5.0 percent), followed by Canada (0.7 percent), while the U.S. GDP increases by only 0.3 percent.

Finally, it should be noted that NAFTA will contribute to a process of North American trade growth, which is already well under way. When Mexico joined GATT in 1986, it was obligated to reduce its general tariff from levels in excess of 80 percent to 50 percent. Mexico went further, unilaterally reducing its average tariff to 10–20 percent. In economic terms, NAFTA will continue this process, but compared with the recent unilateral moves of Mexico, its liberalizing effect will be "at the margin."

NAFTA and the Environment

It is not clear how well pre-NAFTA conditions predict the future of the environment in Mexico and the border region with the United States. NAFTA has been a lightning rod for environmental criticism

TABLE 5. NAFTA IMPACTS: TOTAL IMPORTS AND EXPORTS, ESTIMATED CHANGES IN TRADE RESULTING FROM TARIFF REMOVAL AND QUOTA EXPANSION, AND EFFECTIVE TARIFF LEVELS

Commodity	Total imports* (millions of $)	Change in total imports+ (%)	Total exports (millions of $)	Change in total exports (%)	Effective tariff on imports from U.S. (%)	Effective tariff on imports from Canada (%)	Effective tariff on imports from Mexico (%)
Agricultural, forestry and fish products							
United States	14,010.1	2.0	55,891.4	0.1	—	1.6	4.0
Canada	4,266.3	3.2	11,628.8	0.4	2.2	—	1.8
Mexico	2,288.6	3.2	2,646.1	6.6	2.0	1.1	—
Food, beverages, and tobacco							
United States	29,946.3	1.7	22,300.4	1.9	—	3.8	2.6
Canada	5,649.3	4.6	5,585.7	5.0	5.4	—	5.4
Mexico	1,629.7	12.1	2,057.6	7.4	9.3	1.6	—
Textiles							
United States	8,528.6	0.2	10,145.6	7.7	—	7.2	2.8
Canada	3,167.4	20.6	758.7	5.8	16.9	—	9.1
Mexico	213.8	22.5	669.1	5.6	11.6	11.7	—
Wearing apparel							
United States	10,555.9	1.5	1,942.2	10.0	—	18.4	6.2
Canada	1,168.1	11.3	373.1	31.0	23.7	—	19.8
Mexico	137.8	25.4	460.7	22.9	19.8	19.4	—
Paper and paper products							
United States	10,495.6	0.1	7,435.6	2.4	—	0.0	2.5
Canada	1,262.2	12.0	14,036.4	-0.1	6.6	—	9.9
Mexico	433.5	8.2	107.8	4.6	3.0	2.9	—

Chemicals							
United States	19,173.9	−0.5	36,495.0	3.7	—	0.6	1.2
Canada	7,256.2	12.8	7,170.4	−1.7	7.9	—	8.4
Mexico	2,349.2	15.8	1,426.0	−4.7	7.1	9.8	—
Iron and steel							
United States	16,590.2	1.5	6,719.2	6.5	—	2.7	1.6
Canada	2,872.8	5.4	3,191.8	8.1	5.1	—	0.0
Mexico	2,253.3	13.1	175.5	−5.4	7.5	3.8	—
Metal Products							
United States	10,807.3	2.7	13,356.4	6.0	—	4.0	2.2
Canada	4,567.4	12.9	2,884.7	10.2	8.6	—	10.1
Mexico	991.0	18.2	342.2	1.9	9.6	8.3	—
Nonelectrical machinery							
United States	24,937.6	0.0	56,373.9	3.9	—	2.2	0.9
Canada	16,937.5	7.7	5,515.8	1.4	4.6	—	1.4
Mexico	4,150.2	19.2	714.5	−23.1	12.7	12.1	—
Electrical machinery							
United States	26,843.5	10.0	24,074.6	1.9	—	4.5	2.3
Canada	5,977.1	10.2	2,676.1	10.1	7.5	—	4.9
Mexico	1,372.1	−18.7	2,544.5	100.2	14.2	13.9	—

Sources: D. K. Brown, A. V. Deardorff, and R. M. Stern, "A North American Free Trade Agreement: Analytical Issues and a Computational Assessment," *World Economy*, vol. 15, no. 1(January 1992), pp. 11–29; D. K. Brown, personal communication, June 14, 1993.

*Imports and exports are valued in millions of dollars in 1989.

+Changes in total imports and exports result from removal of tariffs on trade among the United States, Canada, and Mexico, and a 25 percent expansion of U.S. import quotas imposed on Mexican exports of agriculture, food, textiles, and clothing. Changes in imports and exports are valued at fixed 1989 prices.

TABLE 6. ESTIMATED IMPACT OF NAFTA ON GDP

Scenario	Canada		Mexico		United States	
	Absolute change in GDP*	Percent change in GDP	Absolute change in GDP*	Percent change in GDP	Absolute change in GDP*	Percent change in GDP
Reduction of tariffs and nontariff barriers	3.51	0.7	1.98	1.6	6.45	0.1
Reduction of tariffs and nontariff barriers; capital flows into Mexico allowed	3.66	0.7	6.30	5.0	13.23	0.3

Source: D. K. Brown, A. V. Deardorff, and R. M. Stern, "A North American Free Trade Agreement: Analytical Issues and a Computational Assessment," *World Economy*, vol. 15, no. 1 (January 1992), p. 22.

*Billions of U.S. dollars. (The change in GDP was measured in the study as equivalent variation, which is the change in GDP at base period prices that yields the same change in welfare as trade liberalization.)

of trade agreements, largely on the assumption that it will make existing problems worse. Horror stories link conditions in the border region and their associated health effects to serious toxic waste disposal and water treatment problems, and connect these, in turn, to birth defects and other health hazards. These effects have been attributed to trade-related growth, especially of the *maquiladora* factories. Opponents of the agreement project that such problems will continue, and probably worsen, under NAFTA.

Yet without NAFTA, it is doubtful that these problems would have received the attention they have, or that Mexico and the United States would have committed themselves to environmental improvements though enforcement and the negotiation of side agreements. In this sense, while NAFTA may lead to trade patterns with negative environmental effects, it also has created an opportunity to address these effects more openly than ever before. And if it succeeds in generating growth of the sort projected in Mexico, it can create the wherewithal to expand ongoing remedial environmental efforts. Whether such efforts will occur is the focus of the environmental side agreement discussed below. Ironically, if NAFTA had been defeated (on environmental or other grounds), a major opportunity for environmental improvements would have been lost.

With NAFTA passage secured, existing environmental problems in the border region require immediate attention. As industries have expanded, uncontrolled industrial growth, undeveloped infrastructure to deal with industrial, municipal, and animal wastes, and a lack of enforced environmental regulations have resulted in an "environmental disaster zone."[33] Reports have called the U.S.-Mexico border a "virtual cesspool and breeding ground for infectious disease."[34] Factories in Mexico that operate under the *maquiladora* program have been major contributors to the pollution problem. The essential question is whether the *maquiladora* sector is a harbinger of development under NAFTA or will be taken as a warning of what happens when trade is left to expand without accompanying environmental regulation and remediation.

The *maquiladora* program was implemented in Mexico by presidential decree in 1965, and the number of firms operating under the program has grown over 20 percent annually in the last ten years. In 1966 twelve *maquiladora* plants employed 3,000 workers. In 1980 some 119,500 workers were employed in the sector; the number grew to 467,000 workers in 1,925 plants by the end of 1991.[35] The majority of the *maquiladora* plants are owned by U.S. companies, although some have German, Japanese, or other foreign parent companies. Poor enforcement of environmental regulations has resulted in the discharge of toxic wastes and raw sewage from *maquiladora* factories directly into canals and rivers. Waste treatment plants are substandard and often nonexistent. *Maquiladora* factories in Mexico reportedly allow toxic wastes to enter sewage plants without treatment despite the near universality of treatment by the same companies operating in the United States.[36] High levels of smoke and toxic vapors are also discharged into the air. The result of all of these conditions is allegedly higher-than-normal incidences of birth defects, although the evidence is fragmentary.[37]

As trading activities in the border region have created environmental damages, the regulatory response has been widely criticized as insufficient. The most important transnational effort to respond to environmental problems prior to NAFTA was the 1983 La Paz agreement between the United States and Mexico on Cooperation for the Protection and Improvement of the Environment in the Border Area.[38] That agreement includes five annexes, which cover the construction of wastewater treatment facilities in Tijuana and San Diego; contingency planning for hazardous waste spills; transboundary shipment of hazardous wastes; requirements for copper smelters in Arizona, New Mexico, Texas, and Sonora, Mexico, to comply with emission limits; and air emission inventories, air modeling analyses, and other programs aimed at urban air pollution in U.S.-Mexico border cities.[39] The annex relating to transboundary shipment of hazardous wastes requires that any *maquiladora* factories importing toxic chemicals also export the toxic wastes back to the country of origin, since Mexico does not have adequate domestic treatment capacity.

The La Paz agreement has not been strictly enforced, and violations by many *maquiladoras* are documented. For factories in the border region that generate hazardous wastes, the Mexican government reported only a 35 percent compliance rate in 1992 for toxic chemicals paperwork. Many of the toxic chemicals entering

Mexico never return to the United States and are either stored in large quantities in the *maquiladoras* or illegally dumped.[40] In partial response, it has been proposed by various environmental groups that deposits be placed on containers of toxic chemicals when they enter Mexico, to be refunded when the used toxic wastes are returned to the United States.[41]

Following the La Paz agreement, in 1988 the Mexican government enacted the General Law for Ecological Equilibrium and Environmental Protection. This law provides the basis for environmental regulation and enforcement throughout Mexico, and is modeled on U.S. law.[42] While not as detailed as U.S. environmental law, it covers air, water, hazardous waste pollution, pesticides, and toxic chemicals.[43] Under this law, companies seeking to begin operations or make significant changes to their factories must obtain permission from the Secretariat of Social Development (SEDESOL) by submitting a feasibility assessment that details the location and operation planned in Mexico and an environmental impact assessment if environmental risk is deemed significant.[44] However, a lack of financial resources has limited the ability of SEDESOL to enforce environmental legislation and compliance with higher environmental standards.

Prior to the NAFTA side agreement discussions of 1993, the most recent comprehensive regulatory effort in Mexico was the plan adopted jointly by the U.S. Environmental Protection Agency (EPA) and SEDESOL, its Mexican counterpart, in 1992. The Integrated Environmental Plan for the Mexico-U.S. Border Region was initially released in August 1991 and met with much criticism; a revised version was signed by President Bush and President Salinas in March 1992. Infrastructure needs, hazardous wastes, environmental health, and urban development are a few of the issues it addressed. Financial resources and a timetable for implementing changes were also outlined.

The Border Plan and a variety of other Mexican environmental initiatives indicated a strong Mexican desire to raise environmental standards and to begin a more vigorous policy of enforcement, partly in anticipation of the environmental controversy surrounding NAFTA. In late 1991, for example, Mexico began requiring factories with poor environmental records to post performance bonds.[45]

Over a thousand industrial inspections along the U.S.-Mexico border were carried out from June 1991 to June 1992, a substantial increase over earlier enforcement.[46] SEDESOL completely closed down some *maquiladoras* that violated environmental regulations, and forced others to close temporarily.[47] In March 1992 President Salinas demanded that 220 of the most intensive polluters in Mexico City reduce their emissions by 70 percent in eighteen months.[48] At the same time, he announced that companies desiring to open plants in Mexico would be required to complete environmental impact assessments. In May 1992 Salinas reorganized the environmental agencies and promised to improve the infrastructure and environmental conditions along the U.S.-Mexico border, including earmarking $466 million for border environmental projects over the period 1992–1994.[49] These actions were clearly tied to a desire to enhance the prospects of NAFTA's approval. Whether they succeed in permanently regulating Mexico's environment will depend on the financial resources available to the Mexican government to implement and enforce them, which in turn will depend on growth in Mexico's economy, and thus NAFTA itself.

Linked to the discussion of lower environmental standards in Mexico is the concern that the country will attract firms that have high pollution abatement costs at home, becoming a "pollution haven." Firms with high costs of adhering to environmental regulations in the United States may thus have an incentive to relocate where environmental regulations are not as strictly enforced. While these incentives are plausible at first blush, there is no clear consensus as to whether they are great enough to induce firms to relocate. Issues include the relative size of pollution abatement costs, input costs, perceived current and future levels of standards, costs of relocating a firm, and access to inputs and product markets. Firms may also relocate for reasons other than abatement costs, such as cheaper labor and access to markets, and subsequently take advantage of lower environmental standards.

Empirical studies on such relocation bear out the lack of consensus. A survey of such studies found no evidence to support industrial flight and development of pollution havens as a result of a disparity in environmental standards.[50] A 1990 study by economist James Tobey found that twenty-four out of sixty-four U.S. agricultural and manufacturing industries evaluated were pollution-intensive, yet that environmental control costs for these industries amounted to only 1.9–2.9 percent of total costs.[51] Another study, conducted by the World Bank, estimated pollution abatement costs for selected industries in 1988 ranging from 1.03 percent (for industries in miscellaneous primary metal products) to 3.17 percent of value added (for the hydraulic cement industry).[52] Of course, relocation may occur for other reasons and still have environmental implications. And low pollution abatement costs in the United States do not lessen the level of environmental degradation occurring in Mexico, especially in the border region. Although motivations for relocation are complex, there is no reason to delay or reduce efforts to improve environmental compliance in Mexico (or the United States) simply because standards appear to be a small part of total costs. Indeed, there is reason to increase the general level of enforcement not only in Mexico, but in the United States as well.

If Mexico's recent push to improve environmental standards is successful, Mexico is likely to become less of a pollution haven over time. In a 1992 American Chamber of Commerce survey of 125 U.S. companies in Mexico, 90 percent of the respondents reported stricter enforcement of Mexican laws than in past years, and on average participants reported that their environmental control costs had increased by 85 percent.[53] It is noteworthy that although empirical studies fail to show large incentives to relocate for environmental reasons alone, the American Chamber of Commerce survey found that 27 percent of participating companies reported lower environmental costs as an incentive to relocate. In response to a question about the typical technology used to treat industrial wastes, 54 percent stated they used Mexican standards, 29 percent said they used U.S. standards, and 17 percent said they used the best available technology.[54]

In addition to concerns of a Mexican pollution haven and the *maquiladora* pollution problem, other environmental issues arose as NAFTA was negotiated. These included pesticide residues on imported crops and increased levels of air pollution and more toxic spills due to higher levels of traffic. Pesticide standards are a major issue for American consumers. A significant gap exists between U.S.

and Mexican pesticide standards both in legalized pesticide use and in levels of pesticide applications. If pesticide applications in Mexico result in local environmental damage such as groundwater contamination, these damages are a local externality.[55] But when pesticides are applied to crops that are exported, and the exported crops contain harmful pesticide residues, a transnational externality exists.[56] Whether harmonization of standards can effectively confront such an externality or whether the U.S. should restrict market access to these products (with important trade implications under NAFTA and GATT) will remain a troubling issue in relation to the environmental side agreement.

Concern has also risen about the environmental effects of higher levels of traffic resulting from NAFTA, especially in the U.S.-Mexico border region. The standards for vehicle smog emissions are lower in Mexico than in the United States. In addition, truck traffic, which has increased in recent years as trade between the United States and Mexico has grown, is expected to increase further after NAFTA is enacted. If the pollution generated by traffic between the United States, Mexico, and Canada affects all three nations by contributing to poor air quality, or the entire world by contributing to climate change, a global externality exists, requiring multilateral responses, as well as national and trilateral ones.

Institutional Responses to Trade-Environment Conflicts: Side Agreements to NAFTA

In response to a combined desire to promote trade though NAFTA and to assure that it included environmental safeguards (making its passage by Congress more likely), the Clinton administration began a process of trilateral negotiations in March 1993 on an environmental side agreement to the NAFTA text. These negotiations were a precursor of the likely discussion of environmental protection at the multilateral level related to GATT. They had been preceded in the EPA of the Bush administration by considerable efforts to formulate approaches to what eventually became the Clinton side agreement.

In effect, the logic described in chapter 2 (see Figure 1) led the administration and many members of Congress to the following conclusions. First, NAFTA as a trade measure could lead to environmental damages, or at a minimum might aggravate existing environmental conditions, notably in the *maquiladora* sector and border region. Second, remediating these damages required some regulating mechanism, over and above the agreement, to enforce environmental safeguards. Third, since the environmental problems included not only local externalities affecting the home market, but transnational and even global externalities, a coordinated trilateral response was required, involving new institutional authority.

In terms of the principles discussed in chapter 2, NAFTA primarily aims to reduce barriers to trade. If it threatens to create (or fails to reduce) environmental damages, then a separate environmental intervention should be addressed to the problem. This separate interventionary authority took on the form of the trilateral CEC. Environmental groups proposed a variety of responsibilities for the commission, many of which are reflected in the NAFTA side agreement.[57] The CEC will monitor the implementation of NAFTA's environmental provisions, and provide information on compliance with domestic laws in all three countries, regularly reviewing and recommending improvements in compliance and enforcement. In addition, by promoting cooperative trilateral environmental actions, including raising and harmonizing environmental standards, it would help reduce incentives for pollution havens and the use of different standards as nontariff trade barriers. The effectiveness of the CEC will depend on its degree of true oversight authority and its ability to influence, if not control, the flow of funds for trilateral environmental actions. The key challenges facing the CEC are the following.

Active Participation in the Dispute Resolution Process Under NAFTA, dispute resolution through consultation, general meetings of the NAFTA governments, and convening of NAFTA panels will require the active involvement of the CEC. One important role, consistent with the discussion in chapter 2, will be to help determine whether increased trade flows are leading to environmental damages, and to recommend appropriate regulatory responses in the home markets and coordinated trilateral responses in cases of transnational externalities. Alternatively, environmental expertise could help to determine whether different standards imposing trade burdens are justified because they are "primarily aimed at" an environmental target, so that recommendations can be developed that are acceptable in addressing such a target. These forms of influence can occur through direct consultations with the CEC or through "friend of the court" briefs filed with dispute panels or through the NAFTA Trade Commission. The CEC's secretariat (see below) will maintain a roster of environmental experts, analogous to the trade experts roster available to the NAFTA Trade Commission. The scientific and technical skills represented by these experts, together with the secretariat, will assist in making environmental judgments typically beyond the scope of trade policy.

Oversight Reports on Environmental Concerns Related to NAFTA's Implementation An annual CEC report will evaluate the implementation of NAFTA's environmental provisions, and identify where these provisions require supplementation or amendment because of changing policies, circumstances, or knowledge (for example, passage of a U.S. energy tax). In addition, it will serve to remind and occasionally embarrass national (and state and local) governments when lax enforcement or a lowering of standards occurs.

Enforcement and Levying of Fines A controversial area involves the power directly to enforce compliance with environmental regulations or to levy fines or sanctions (including trade sanctions) for noncompliance. In the final and difficult side agreement negotiations, this matter was left in such a way that fines would apply to Canadian actions, while sanctions applied to Mexico and the United States.[58] These powers raise questions of jurisdictionality (see the discussion of the tuna-dolphin case in chapter 4) and thus of sovereignty. However, it is also clear that without "teeth" and financial powers of some sort, the effectiveness of the CEC will be in question.

Assistance in Implementing NAFTA's Environmental Provisions, and in Developing Additional Supplementary Agreements Examples of the CEC's potential role in implementing NAFTA's environmental provisions include clarifying the relationship between NAFTA and international environmental agreements such as the Montreal Protocol, and assisting in the application of NAFTA's food safety and other technical standards so that they lead to upward harmonization and discourage pollution havens.[59] If and when amendments to NAFTA are made, or additional countries join the agreement, the CEC can also assist in bringing existing environmental provisions to bear or adding needed supplementary language.

Serving as a Source of Information and "Sounding Board" on North American Environmental Issues An important concern in the environmental community is the perceived lack of access and of information concerning trade-environment linkages offered by government trade ministers. An important role of the CEC will be to make these linkages more "transparent," affording greater access and participation in trade and environmental policymaking. The Rio Declaration on Environment and Development, adopted in June 1992, established as principle 10 that "each individual shall have appropriate access to information concerning the environment that is held by public authorities, including information on hazardous materials and activities in their communities, and the opportunity to participate in the decision making process."[60]

In sections relating to public participation and dispute settlement, the CEC and its secretariat are empowered to act on submissions to develop fact-finding reports to be made public, subject to a two-to-one majority.[61] In order to carry out these specific functions, the CEC requires a well-defined organizational structure. When originally proposed by the Bush administration, the CEC was to be composed of the three national environment ministers, who would meet annually or semiannually. The August 1993 side agreement developed a more detailed structure. The CEC includes the Council of Parties, comprising cabinet-level environmental and health officials meeting in regular session, the central secretariat, and the Joint Public Advisory Committee. The side agreement elaborates the functions of the council, the secretariat, and the advisory committee, and specifies the obligations for annual reporting and notification and provision of information.[62]

A final question concerns the financial resources necessary to conduct the business of the CEC. Several environmental groups have proposed a "cross-border tax," or the earmarking of tariff revenues (which would decline as NAFTA phases them down or out), together with collections from fees, penalties, and the issuance of bonds.[63] While measures such as the cross-border tax have been opposed as a reversion to protectionism, there is a logical basis for applying the "polluter pays principle" in such a way as to generate revenues for environmental protection.[64] However, the more broadly taxes or fees are levied, the less consistent they are with the principle. The more clearly targeted to polluters (for example, through penalties for noncompliance), the more consistent they are, but the less reliable they become as a continuing revenue source. Determining the appropriate mix of revenue-generating policies and how to implement such a scheme is one of the most contentious issues affecting the future of the CEC.

Nevertheless, the basic structure of the CEC appears to offer an important prototype for broader international efforts to link trade and environmental policies. As in the process of integration in the EU, the tension between the subsidiarity of national interests and the need for an overarching institutional authority such as the CEC is the critical institutional balancing question for NAFTA. Whether the new NAFTA Environment Commission can achieve the legitimacy granted to the European institutions responsible for the environment remains an open question. If the CEC is established with well-defined oversight authority, technical competence, and responsibility for ongoing evaluation of trade and environmental interactions, it and the EU can offer models that may also be applicable to the future of the multilateral trade system and GATT. These institutional issues will remain relevant, and will be taken up in chapter 6.

Chapter 4

Environmental Measures and Trade

In contrast to the environmental community's concern over the impacts of more liberal trade, those most directly involved in trade policy have generally focused on the potential for protectionism disguised as environmental action. This can occur when a country or trading bloc protects internal markets in the name of environmental health or safety. It can also occur when higher levels of environmental standards are used to bar market access to goods and services produced under lower levels of regulation, especially by developing countries. Two cases are examined here: the tuna-dolphin dispute between the United States and Mexico, and a less well-known dispute between the United States and Canada over fisheries regulation. These cases show that sorting out protectionism from sound environmental policy involves complex legal, scientific, and institutional issues.

THE TUNA-DOLPHIN DISPUTE

Perhaps the most divisive and inflammatory case of trade versus environmental interests arose from the 1991 tuna-dolphin dispute between the United States, Mexico, and several other countries. The dispute illustrates the problem of transnational and global externalities, and the complex jurisdictional issues in dealing with them.

It also illustrates how GATT, in attempting to prevent trade distortions, can easily be cast as an environmental villain. Because of the complexity of such cases, it is often difficult to understand how they are decided. This discussion is designed to provide a basis for such understanding, although many question whether the decision in the tuna-dolphin case is well grounded, even within the narrow confines of GATT law.

In September 1991 a GATT dispute resolution panel ruled that a U.S. ban on imports of tuna violated GATT rules.[1] The ruling was against a U.S. law that attempted to protect dolphins that followed schools of tuna and were thus often caught and killed in the purse seine nets used to harvest tuna. Many members of the environmental community and Congress interpreted the panel's decision as evidence that GATT rules could be used to undermine and even overturn domestic efforts to protect international environmental resources and could weaken international environmental agreements such as the Montreal Protocol.

The dispute itself arose from a challenge by Mexico to provisions of the U.S. Marine Mammal Protection Act of 1972 (MMPA)[2] limiting incidental killing or serious injury to dolphins and other marine mammals in the course of commercial fishing activities. Specifically, the MMPA required trade embargoes of yellowfin tuna from any nation whose average catch of dolphin incidental to tuna harvesting in the Eastern Tropical Pacific (ETP) exceeded a prescribed limit. This limit was set at 1.25 times the average incidental catch of the U.S. fleet in the ETP in the same year. The MMPA also required "secondary embargoes" on all tuna-importing and tuna-exporting nations that did not ban imports of tuna from the nations covered by the primary embargo within sixty days of its imposition by the United States. At the time of Mexico's challenge, Venezuela and Vanuatu were also subject to primary embargoes.[3]

The GATT panel upheld Mexico's challenge,[4] finding that the MMPA embargo constituted a quantitative import restriction, prohibited by GATT article XI; the embargo was not imposed in conjunction with an internal restriction as called for under article III (since the MMPA regulated the *process* of tuna harvesting rather than the tuna itself); the embargo was not "necessary," as the United States claimed, "to protect human, animal, or plant life or health"; and the embargo was not justified as "relating to the conservation of exhaustible natural resources."[5] The fact that the embargo was not found "necessary" also related to the argument that GATT does not permit *extrajurisdictional* measures to protect animal life or health; that the United States had not exhausted other, *less trade-restrictive* remedies; and that the U.S. dolphin catch restrictions were contingent and unpredictable, since the ratio of 1.25 times the U.S. fleet catch would rise and fall with the catch itself, and the resulting limit could not be known until the end of the period in question.[6]

These GATT legalisms raise three key issues of general relevance to trade and the environment. First, was the attempt to use trade measures to achieve an environmental objective (namely, to reduce the killing of dolphins during tuna harvests), an example of appropriate, or inappropriate, "cross-matching" of trade and environmental instruments? Second, the panel ruling (which has not been agreed to by the parties, and probably will not be) seemed to indicate that GATT's exceptions for health, and the conservation of natural resources, do not cover extrajurisdictional measures designed to protect against transnational or global externalities, including international environmental agreements. Third, is the important product-process distinction (between barriers imposed on *products* versus on the *process* by which these products are made), which the panel employed in arguing against the U.S. embargoes.

"Cross-Matching" Trade and Environmental Instruments

In its concluding remarks, the panel emphasized that GATT allows considerable leeway for governments to undertake *domestic* measures to protect the environment from local externalities. However, when transnational or global externalities are involved, the panel argued, a party is not permitted to restrict imports of a product because it originates from a country with environmental policies that differ from those of the importer. Nevertheless, many in the environmental community felt that trade barriers were justified to achieve environmental targets, especially where transnational or global externalities were at stake. Strict application of the panel's reasoning would render ineffective environmental policies that attempt to use trade as a "stick." On the other side, the trade community argued that allowing such cross-matching of trade and environmental instruments would cause a slide down a slippery slope of protectionism in "green disguise." The GATT secretariat, in its 1992 analysis of trade and the environment, presented this argument forcefully.[7] The tuna-dolphin dispute thus brought into sharp relief the contrasting views of the environment and trade communities.

On the environment side, the primary concern was that the panel ruling could be used to argue that other provisions of U.S. law, in which trade measures are used for environmental purposes, also violate GATT. These include the Packwood and Pelly Amendments, which are designed to enforce the Convention for the Regulation of Whaling through restrictions on fishing allocation rights within the U.S. fishery conservation zone if the secretary of commerce determines that foreign nationals "diminish the effectiveness" of the Convention.[8] They also include the Endangered Species Act of 1973, which prohibits trade in endangered species, and the African Elephant Conservation Act,[9] which prohibits ivory imports from countries with inadequate elephant conservation programs. Finally, related to the Montreal Protocol are provisions of the Clean Air Act[10] that restrict imports and exports of ozone-depleting chemicals. It is argued that if countries such as the United States cannot exercise the leverage of market access, then a powerful mechanism for inducing countries with weaker levels of environmental protection to raise their standards is lost.

From the trade perspective, these fears attached too much significance to the GATT panel's views. First, the tuna-dolphin panel ruling is unlikely to be agreed to, since Mexico has chosen to pursue settlement negotiations with the United States rather than to push the GATT ruling body to adopt the report. Second, as Jackson has argued, panel reports, even when adopted, are binding on the disputants as to how the particular case in question shall be resolved, but provide no formal precedent.[11] These observations have offered little reassurance to the environmental community, however, since GATT panel rulings are widely used to document arguments for and against certain types of trade measures.

As noted in chapter 2, if an environmental measure is indeed a barrier to trade (which in the case of an embargo is clear), then whether this is justified depends on balancing its environmental benefits against its costs of trade distortion. The panel made two such judgments in this case, the "necessary" test and the "primarily aimed at" test. In the case of the "necessary" test, the panel argued that the United States had not demonstrated alternative attempts to negotiate international cooperative agreements to protect dolphins.[12] If such an "alternative measure" was available "which [the nation] could reasonably be expected to employ and which is not inconsistent with other GATT provisions, then the measure employed was not necessary."[13] The particular interpretation given to the "necessary" test—the "least GATT-inconsistent" measure available—was widely criticized for being too open-ended, since any measure might have hypothetical alternatives that are more in keeping with GATT. A similar problem arises if "necessary" mutates to a "least-restrictive" test.[14] The panel also found that U.S. law "could not be regarded as being primarily aimed at the conservation of dolphins,"[15] since the type of standard used (1.25 times catch rates) could be set unilaterally by any country for protectionist purposes.

However, the United States was in fact involved in ongoing international attempts to resolve the issue by alternative means, through the Inter-American Tropical Tuna Commission (IATTC), established in 1949. In April and June of 1992, the IATTC, representing all of the principal nations engaged in fishing in the ETP, agreed to the following:

- Mandatory, progressive reduction in the level of dolphin mortality in the ETP by all IATTC participants

- A review panel responsible for monitoring and reporting on compliance with the mandatory dolphin mortality reductions

- A research program designed to discover and develop modifications to current technology that reduce dolphin deaths, and new technologies for catching mature tuna that do not involve dolphin

- A scientific advisory board of technical specialists responsible for reviewing, recommending, and helping to seek funding for specific research plans

Both the review panel and the scientific advisory board include representatives of environmental organizations. However, the IATTC agreement does not authorize trade sanctions as a means of enforcing its dolphin mortality reduction requirements. If the agreement were amended to include such an authorization, it would supersede GATT rules with respect to the IATTC participants.[16]

In addition to these negotiations, the United States was engaged in efforts to amend domestic laws in order to aim more accurately at the environmental target of dolphin protection.[17] On October 8, 1992, the Senate unanimously passed its version of a House bill that would significantly amend the MMPA's tuna-dolphin provisions. The Bush administration actively endorsed the bill (H.R. 5419) as a solution to the tuna-dolphin dispute and the issues raised by the panel report on the MMPA embargo, and President Bush signed it into law (Public Law 102-523). The new MMPA amendments offer relief from the existing MMPA embargo provisions for any nation that agrees to adopt a five-year moratorium on tuna fishing in association with dolphin in the ETP as of March 1, 1994. Such relief is contingent on the foreign nation's commitment to reduce "significantly" its incidental dolphin catch in the ETP prior to March 1, 1994, and to engage in an international program of dolphin-protection research. Violations of these commitments, however, would trigger severe U.S. sanctions: an import ban on all yellowfin tuna and yellowfin tuna products; if noncompliance continues for sixty days after imposition of the tuna embargo, an additional import ban would be imposed on *any or all* other fish and fish products.

The new amendments also flatly prohibit, as of June 1, 1994, any U.S. trade (domestic or international) in tuna that is not considered "dolphin-safe" under U.S. law. Dolphin-safe tuna, as defined by the Dolphin Protection Consumer Information Act, is tuna caught on a fishing trip involving no sets of nets on dolphin, regardless of whether the tuna at issue was caught in such a set.

Whether this new ban on trade in non–dolphin-safe tuna is justifiable under GATT will merit close consideration. The new law allows parties to escape an embargo, but only at a price of accepting an agreement that is more stringent than the MMPA, and with more severe penalties. To many critics of the heavy hand of U.S. policy, this is hardly an accommodation to GATT norms.[18]

Health and Environmental Exceptions, Extrajurisdictionality, and International Environmental Agreements

The GATT exceptions for health and environmental policies, which allow countries to pursue such policies even if they lead to trade barriers, have been interpreted narrowly, and the tuna-dolphin decision continued the practice. The Office of Technology Assessment of the U.S. Congress has noted that of all dispute resolution panel reports from 1947 to 1990, nine involved these types of exceptions. Of the nine, two did not contain a ruling on their applicability, six found that they did not apply, and only one found that they did.[19] Thus, GATT panel rulings offer little documentation to support the argument that environmental measures that impose trade burdens are subject to these exceptions, but more documentation supporting the claim that they do not apply or are not a basis for an exception.

The tuna-dolphin panel stated that the exceptions for policies designed to protect life or health or natural resources apply only "within the jurisdiction of the importing country." Since the dolphins in the ETP were outside the jurisdiction of the United States, the panel reasoned that the exceptions did not apply.[20] If the GATT exceptions apply only to measures designed to mitigate local externalities, but may not extend to transnational or global cases in which measures imposing trade burdens reach beyond one's own country, then the extrajurisdictional reach necessary to enforce them appears to come into direct conflict with GATT law.[21]

Considerable disagreement, however, surrounds whether the panel's interpretation is supported by the drafting history of article XX, which contains the exceptions to which the panel referred. Legal scholar Jeffrey Dunoff notes that article XX is based on the exceptions clause of the Draft Charter of the International Trade Organization (ITO) in 1946. The records of the 1946 Draft Charter provide no evidence "that even hints that nations are limited to protecting animal or plant life within its [sic] border," nor are the exceptions "intended to disable nations from protecting global commons resources through the use of green trade barriers." Steve

Charnovitz, another student of article XX, points out that "trade treaties have provided exceptions for the protection of humans, animals and plants since the late 19th century."[22] The 1927 exceptions to the International Convention for the Abolition of Import and Export Prohibitions and Restrictions, from which the GATT exceptions were drawn, include measures to preserve animals and plants from "degeneration or extinction." This language was included to ensure that "abolition" was not taken to apply to contemporaneous controls on imports of birds, seals, salmon, halibut, wildlife trophies, and other international environmental measures that dealt with transnational and global externalities. In short:

> It is sometimes suggested that the GATT's authors never contemplated extrajurisdictional use. A better interpretation . . . is that they understood that Article XX(b) would apply to extrajurisdictional measures, but considered that point so obvious that it did not engender debate. Certainly, the record fails to show anyone at the UN Conference suggesting that Article XX(b) should *not* apply extrajurisdictionally. Moreover, it seems evident that the United States—whose 1946 draft of Article XX(b) emerged unscathed in the GATT—perceived its text as covering U.S. import prohibitions in effect at that time, which included extrajurisdictional measures.[23]

The tuna-dolphin panel also rejected the application of the GATT exceptions on the basis of a particular interpretation of the "primarily aimed at" test. It reasoned that since a country can restrict production and consumption only when they are under its jurisdiction, measures primarily aimed at accomplishing this task cannot be extrajurisdictional, and thus the exceptions cannot refer to such cases. But this fails to consider the role of trade measures that affect other countries' imports (of non–dolphin-safe tuna) and thus reduce *consumption* (of such tuna) in the home market.[24] Few doubt that the MMPA was primarily aimed at the protection of marine mammals, but if it applied only to the U.S. fishing fleet, it would have had limited effect.[25]

In summary, the GATT tuna-dolphin panel's claims against the MMPA trade measures designed to make environmental regulations effective have met with general dissatisfaction. That the exceptions in GATT, if applied to include such regulations, would lead down the "slippery slope" of "green protectionism" is the offsetting argument of many in the trade community.

Process Versus Product

A third question the tuna-dolphin panel raised is the distinction between trade barriers imposed on products and those imposed on particular production processes. The panel rejected the U.S. claim that the MMPA incidental-taking requirements for tuna were "an internal regulation enforced at the point of importation."[26] The reason for the panel's rejection was that the MMPA embargo was unrelated to the characteristics of the product (yellowfin tuna), but discriminated instead against the production process. The panel reasoned that "Article III requires a comparison between products of the exporting and importing nations, and not a comparison between different nations' production processes that have no effect on the product *qua* product."[27]

There is considerable disagreement between the trade and environmental communities over whether allowing such "process" arguments will again lead to a "slippery slope," in which, as the GATT secretariat has warned, "access to one's own market [becomes] dependent on the domestic environmental policies or practices of the exporting country."[28] If, for example, the U.S. government feels that workers manufacturing automobiles or growing crops in foreign countries are exposed to substantial health hazards or that exhaustible natural resources are threatened in the process, should this constitute a basis for import levies or prohibitions against such products, even if the autos and crops themselves pose no such threats?

Trade policy experts perceive a Pandora's box of problems, including the following examples:

- An importing country prohibits the sale of radios, whether domestic or imported, that are produced by workers who are paid less than a minimum wage specified by the importing country. This minimum might be the importing country's own minimum wage, or it might be an amount considerably less but still substantial (in a poor country's economy).

- An importing country that prohibits women from working in certain types of manufacturing plants also prohibits the importation of goods produced in similar plants that utilize women employees.

- An importing country that specifies a weekly religious holiday—for example, Saturday or Sunday—prohibits the importation of goods produced by work on the specified religious holiday.[29]

While such examples may seem extreme, they are the logical consequence of widespread process bans.

The Tuna-Dolphin Case: Summary

In the final analysis, the tuna-dolphin case rests on the perceived legitimacy, or illegitimacy, of using trade instruments for environmental objectives. The trade-off is that the use of such instruments for such purposes poses substantial risks of creating a "green" disguise for trade barriers. As Jackson states, the GATT

> . . . must give specific and significant attention to this trade-off in order to provide for exceptions for environmental purposes. The exceptions should have well-established boundaries so as to prevent them from being used as excuses for a variety of protectionist devices or unilateral social welfare concerns.[30]

It is these "boundaries" that the tuna-dolphin dispute raised as an issue, but did little to resolve, especially in contrast to the case heard before a U.S.-Canada panel on salmon and herring fisheries. This case is our next subject.

U.S.-CANADA: SALMON AND HERRING LANDING REQUIREMENTS

In contrast to the tuna-dolphin panel decision, the 1989 dispute between the United States and Canada over landing requirements for salmon and herring offers an example of the synthesis of law, economics, and environmental perspectives. Salmon from many stocks swim into and out of the territorial waters of both the United States and Canada, making them a transnational resource, with many global commons property characteristics.[31] The conservation of this exhaustible resource requires that governments, including those of Canada and the United States, restrict fishing rights so as to maximize the harvest of abundant stocks and minimize harvest of depleted or threatened stocks. These objectives are translated into restrictive policies based on catch data.[32] It was the manner in which data were gathered for these estimates (through 100 percent sampling of catch) that led to the U.S. complaint.

A panel was convened under the Canadian-U.S. Free Trade Agreement to hear testimony concerning a Canadian requirement that salmon and herring caught in Canadian waters off the west coast of Canada be landed at Canadian counting stations. The landing requirement was a successor to a 1908 ban on exports of unprocessed salmon and herring, which was found GATT-illegal in 1987 after the United States complained that it was an unjustifiable restriction on trade. In 1988 Canada accepted the GATT finding, but stated that it would substitute a landing requirement in order to permit inspection of the catch. The ostensible reason for the requirement was an environmental one: to allow the fish harvest to be counted and monitored so as to preserve the fishery from over-exploitation.

According to the United States, the requirement that all fish first be landed in Canada constituted an export restriction in violation of GATT article XI:1 because of the extra time and expense U.S. buyers must incur in landing and unloading, including dockage fees and product deterioration. The Canadians held that their landing requirement was not an export restraint at all, and thus not subject to GATT rules. Alternatively, they argued that they were pursuing "conservation and management goals" for five varieties of salmon (some of which had previously not been covered by the export ban), as well as herring, so that even if the landing requirement were an export restriction under GATT, it was justified under article XX(g), the exception for conservation of exhaustible natural resources.[33]

The United States contended that although the new herring and salmon regulations "are carefully worded to avoid the appearance of creating direct export prohibitions or restrictions, their clear effect is to restrict exports."[34] As for the conservation defense, the United States argued that the Canadian landing requirement was not "primarily aimed at" the conservation of salmon and herring stocks, the interpretation given to article XX(g) by the 1987 GATT ruling. Thus, the United States held that the Canadian landing requirement was a disguised restriction on international trade—a trade restriction posing as an environmental policy measure. Canada countered that the landing requirement was in fact primarily aimed at the conservation of the salmon and herring fisheries.

In a significant decision, the panel found that if the effect of such a measure is to impose a materially greater commercial burden on exports than on domestic sales, it amounts to a restriction on trade in violation of article XI:1, whether or not its trade effects can be quantitatively demonstrated. The panel was satisfied that the cost of complying with the landing requirement would be more than an insignificant extra expense for those buyers who would have otherwise shipped directly from the fishing grounds to a landing site in the United States. With regard to the conservation exception, the panel was conscious of the need to allow governments appropriate latitude in implementing their environmental policies, and that the trade interests of one state should not be allowed to override the legitimate environmental concerns of another. If the measure would have been adopted for conservation reasons alone, the panel said, the GATT exceptions permit a government the freedom to employ it. The exceptions under GATT article XX were given a less narrow interpretation here than in the tuna-dolphin decision.

This interpretation led the panel to two conclusions. First, "since governments do not adopt conservation measures unless the benefits to conservation are worth the costs," the magnitude of costs to the parties in the form of commercial disadvantage must be examined. Second, "how genuine the conservation purpose of a measure is, must be determined by whether the government would have been prepared to adopt that measure *if its own nationals had to bear the actual costs of the measure*."[35] In this case, the panel was unconvinced that the measure would have been imposed if Canadian interests had been the ones to bear the extra costs. Alternative methods of effectively monitoring catch rates, which posed far fewer commercial burdens, were available.

The U.S.-Canada salmon-herring case provides four lessons useful in sorting out whether environmental measures are justified when they burden international trade. First, it illustrates a clear line of reasoning from a finding of trade burden to a justification for the burden in terms of environmental protection under the GATT exceptions for the conservation of exhaustible natural resources. Second, it offers an interpretation of the "primarily aimed at" test that is more precise than the "necessary" tests discussed in the tuna-dolphin case. Third, it gives a benefit-cost interpretation to the balancing judgment whether the burden of an environmental measure on trade is justified by its environmental (including non-economic) advantages. Fourth, it offers a practical way of deciding how important these environmental advantages are as compared with trade effects, thus helping to determine whether the measure is primarily aimed at environmental targets or is a disguised barrier to trade.

Finding of a Burden on Trade

The panel's line of reasoning was divided into a finding that a burden on trade existed because of the salmon and herring landing requirements in violation of article XI:1 and a judgment that this burden was not justified under the conservation exceptions of article XX(g). The finding of burden arose from the requirement that roe herring and sockeye, pink coho, chum, and chinook salmon caught commercially in Canadian waters be offloaded at licensed "fish landing stations" in British Columbia, or onto a vessel or vehicle destined for such stations. Canada's Department of Fisheries and Oceans used these stations to count and examine the catch in order to set limits and restrictive policies for future catch rates.

The United States contended that the requirement that 100 percent of its catch be landed and counted was an export restriction, proscribed under article XI of GATT, which is incorporated implicitly in article 407 of the Canadian-U.S. Trade Agreement of 1989.[36] The panel agreed that a requirement to land in Canada posed an additional burden on the U.S. buyers, rejecting Canada's claim that U.S. buyers were free to procure fish under the same terms and conditions as Canadian buyers. Even through the landing measure did not apply specifically to exports, it had the effect of imposing costs on U.S. export sales not borne by most Canadian buyers, acting as a restriction not only on "exportation," but on "sale for export" as well, as stated in article XI:1. The panel stated that "the concept of 'sale for export' extends the coverage of article XI:1 to restrictions imposed at an earlier stage in the process, before the act of exportation itself."[37] Hence, on balance, the panel found evidence that a burden to trade existed under article XI:1, because "the cost of complying with the landing requirement would be more than an insignificant expense for those buyers who would have otherwise shipped directly from the fishing ground to a landing site in the United States."[38]

Justifying the Burden: The "Primarily Aimed At" Test

Given the determination of such a burden, the next question was whether the burden was justified. In this case, the justification Canada relied on was the conservation exception under GATT article XX(g), relating to exhaustible natural resources. Canada was required to show that the landing requirements were *primarily aimed at* such conservation; if not, then they were instead a disguised restriction on international trade. This choice of criteria for justifying an environmental measure explicitly avoided the pitfalls of the "necessary" test and its various mutations. In applying the test, the panel relied on the 1987 GATT ruling against Canada, which stated that "while a trade measure did not have to be necessary or essential to the conservation of an exhaustible natural resource, it had to be primarily aimed at the conservation of an exhaustible natural resource to be considered as 'relating to' conservation within the meaning of article XX(g)."[39] The panel argued that if such a measure was found to be primarily aimed at an environmental objective, ipso facto, it could not be a disguised restriction to international trade.[40]

How is this test to be applied? First, in contrast to the narrow scope for article XX exceptions suggested in the tuna-dolphin case, here the panel offered relatively wide latitude for conservation goals at which a party might take aim, including both "economic and noneconomic interests." This interpretation allows article XX to protect the trade interests of one state from overriding "the legitimate environmental concerns of another."[41] At the same time, the panel did not suggest that such exceptions apply to all trade-distorting measures that are given a "green" cast. Rather, it proposed an objective assessment of the measure:

> A measure such as the Canadian landing requirement might achieve several effects including both a conservation-promoting and a trade-restricting effect. But even so, this would not exclude the existence of a

genuine conservation objective. The measure in question could be a valuable part of a conservation programme, worth doing for conservation reasons alone.[42]

Benefits and Costs

The objective assessment proposed in balancing the benefits of an environmental measure against the burdens imposed on trade is a benefit-cost assessment. This assessment, it bears emphasis, does not require quantitative computation of all benefits (which may be noneconomic or quasi-economic, such as species preservation). Nor does it demand exact calculation of all costs (which may be equally difficult to estimate). As the panel noted, citing other decisions in GATT, measurable trade distortions may require "data to show what would have happened without the measure and GATT decisions have not required such proof. What has to be shown is that the measure has altered the competitive relationship between foreign and domestic buyers."[43]

In effect, the balancing judgment required by the "primarily aimed at" test, while difficult and subject to disagreement, is not logically forbidding, and can be applied in a wide variety of examples in which environmental measures affect trade. The judgment is to weigh the costs in the alteration of the competitive relationship between foreign and domestic interests against the benefits of the environmental measure. Especially where these benefits are not in debate or a reasonable consensus exists on environmental goals, the issue becomes one of minimizing the costs in the form of distortions to trade while holding to these goals. This is an application of the principles for trade described in chapter 2.

Giving Additional Priority to Environmental Benefits

Because environmental benefits are notoriously difficult to measure, and often depend on noneconomic values, objective assessments of the "primarily aimed at" test need to rely on unpriced values revealed by countries' actions in formulating environmental policies.[44] The litmus test offered by the panel in the U.S.-Canada case was whether the landing requirements imposed on the United States would have been undertaken by Canada if their burdens had fallen wholly on its own nationals.

In other words, how genuine the conservation purpose of a measure is, must be determined by whether the government would have been prepared to adopt that measure if its own nationals had to bear the actual costs of the measure.

. . . the issue must be posed in terms of whether Canada would have adopted the landing requirement if that measure had required an equivalent number of Canadian buyers to land and unload elsewhere than at their intended destination.[45]

If a procedure imposing lower costs on exporters could be implemented by requiring less onerous landing requirements and still provide sufficient data, the panel argued, then the article XX exception would not justify the 100 percent landing regulation.[46]

The Salmon-Herring Case: Summary

The U.S.-Canada salmon-herring case suggests a general method by which to interpret exceptions to GATT that justify certain environmental measures even if trade burdens result. The "primarily aimed at" test is given a benefit-cost interpretation that is not strictly economic, but allows reasonable criteria to be applied to determine the scope of environmental exceptions. Specifically, it suggests that if the cost of the environmental measure in terms of trade losses would be undertaken even if these losses were fully borne in the home market, then the revealed national importance of the measure in environmental terms can be assumed, and its adverse effects on trade may be tolerated. If not, then the test suggests a search for other ways of accomplishing the environmental purpose that are less trade-distorting.

Despite the important implications of the panel's decision, several caveats are in order. First, the panel's benefit-cost distinction was conclusory and involved no detailed analytical accounting. Panels are relatively weak institutions and are unlikely to undertake such analytical exercises, nor should they be expected to do so. Supplementary analysis by environmental and trade experts will therefore probably be necessary. Second, the conclusions of the panel were made easier by the clear discrepancy in this case between the questionable environmental benefits of counting 100 percent of catch (versus, say, 80 percent) and the costs of doing so in terms of trade distortion. In cases that are less clear-cut, the importance of analysis will loom far larger, and the dispute settlement panel will depend on the input of environmental expertise from outside. Third, the need for outside assistance emphasizes the need for institutional mechanisms to guarantee appropriate input, such as provided for under the CEC resulting from the NAFTA side agreement.

Chapter 5

Trade Obligations and International Environmental Agreements: The Montreal Protocol

In the last decade, a variety of new multilateral agreements have been negotiated in response to several global environmental challenges, including ozone depletion, species extinction, protection of Antarctica, and international management of the oceans. The United Nations Conference on Environment and Development, held in Rio de Janeiro in June 1992, resulted in a broad new mandate for environmental action, Agenda 21, together with the creation of the new UN Commission on Sustainable Development. Almost all of these agreements require their signatories to refrain from trade in certain goods or processes. NAFTA negotiations created a trinational commission with limited authority over trade with damaging environmental effects. The questions are: How are these international environmental accords to be balanced with existing or new trade obligations? What body of international law, and which international institutions, should exercise authority over the intersection between multilateral environmental and trade policy?

The evolution of the world trading system in goods and services has led to international recognition of the need for rules to guide and discipline these commercial transactions. GATT, created in 1947, has steadily grown in the number of contracting parties, from twenty-two at its inception to 117 today. GATT rules have been expanded through additional codes to cover standards and subsidies; with the Uruguay Round concluded, the rules will also extend to services and agriculture.

Just as the maturation and integration of trade in goods and services led to the recognized need for such rules, so the growing recognition that trade involves "bads," such as pollution and hazardous wastes, suggests the need for rules to guide and discipline these damages. The result has been a growing number of international agreements affecting the environment. The UNEP's *Register* lists 152 multilateral agreements (including protocols and amendments) on environmental issues up to 1990, of which 102 had been concluded since 1970.[1] These agreements constitute only the beginning of a burgeoning legal and economic effort to provide rules for environmental interactions among nations and commercial actors. The proliferation of these multilateral or international environmental agreements has raised important questions over their relationship to trade agreements, notably GATT. Among the most ambitious and important examples of such an environmental measure is the Montreal Protocol on Substances that Deplete the Ozone Layer.

The ozone layer is concentrated from six to thirty miles above the earth's surface, and absorbs much of the ultraviolet radiation from the sun. This radiation, if unfiltered by the ozone layer, would be very harmful to life on earth, causing radiation-related changes in plant and animal life, including skin diseases in humans and a variety of mutations in plants and animals. Protecting the ozone is thus in the interest of the global commons. Unfortunately, strong scientific evidence links deterioration of the ozone layer to certain trace gases and other by-products of a variety of industrial processes. The first of these to be recognized was a large class of chemicals known as chlorofluorocarbons. CFCs are broken down by ultraviolet radiation in a way that causes a thinning in the ozone layer, allowing ultraviolet light to penetrate it more easily. CFCs have been widely used in aerosol cans as a propellant, in refrigeration equipment, as a blowing agent for foam fillings, and as a solvent. While sales of CFCs peaked in the United States in the mid-1970s, sales in the rest of the world continued to climb until the mid-1980s, when use began to decline to levels close to those of the 1970s.

Growing scientific evidence since the late 1970s suggests that a 1 percent increase in ultraviolet radiation is likely to be associated with a 5 percent increase in nonmalignant skin diseases, and perhaps a 1 percent increase in malignancies. One estimate is that if no controls were put on CFCs, 3 million additional deaths from nonmalignant skin disease and 200,000 additional deaths from skin cancer could occur in the United States before the year 2075.[2] CFCs are also associated with global warming, and may lead to suppression of human and animal immune systems, and to an increase in parasitic and viral infection.

In 1978 the United States banned the use of CFCs in aerosols. Despite this ban, it became increasingly obvious in the face of the health impacts of ozone depletion that coordinated multilateral actions were necessary. In response, in 1985 the Convention for the Protection of the Ozone Layer was drawn up by the major negotiating parties in Vienna, although neither consensus nor scientific proof was achieved until later. In 1987 all major CFC-producing countries signed the Montreal Protocol, which took effect at the beginning of 1989. The Montreal Protocol called for a freeze on the consumption of CFCs by mid-1990, a 20 percent reduction of consumption by mid-1994, and an additional 30 percent reduction by 1999. Thus a 50 percent reduction in consumption was to be achieved by the end of the century.

In contrast, it permitted *production* to increase by 10 percent from a 1986 base until 1990, but called for it to fall to 90 percent of the 1986 base by 1994 and to 65 percent by 1999. The distinction between consumption and production was critical to the agreement, because it allowed developing countries some flexibility in expanding consumption within limits (namely, though refrigeration). In 1990 the London Amendments expanded the coverage of the agreement.

In sum, the Montreal Protocol was achieved in stages. The 1985 Vienna Convention,[3] which provided for general policy goals but no quantitative restrictions on substances that were shown to deplete the ozone layer over Antarctica, was deemed inadequate in the face of mounting evidence of ozone depletion. The 1987 Protocol added quantitative restrictions, but it was the 1990 London Amendments[4] that added an annex to stabilize and eventually reduce chemicals not covered under the existing annex. Together, the 1987 Protocol and 1990 London Amendments were comprehensive attempts to mobilize multilateral actions to reduce environmental damages affecting the global commons of the earth's atmosphere. However, the commitments undertaken bind only those states that accept them, and may be adjusted to include further binding reductions for controlled substances only by a qualified majority of the parties.[5]

For this discussion, the most important aspect of the Montreal Protocol is that it applies pressure to countries to sign the agreement by restricting and eventually prohibiting parties from *trading* in the controlled substances with nonparties.[6] Also, its commitments to aid developing countries in converting away from ozone-depleting technologies through a fund devoted to new technology transfers would affect the flow of trade. Finally, it included limited provisions to allow trade in quotas for production of restricted substances to promote "industrial rationalization."[7] In short, the Montreal Protocol explicitly calls for measures that may impose burdens on trade, and that therefore are potentially in conflict with the GATT articles.

The dilemma for the trading system is that it is difficult to conceive of how an agreement such as the Montreal Protocol can succeed without certain burdensome trade measures, especially import restrictions on products (and processes) hazardous to the ozone layer. These restrictions can help persuade nonsignatories to join the Protocol; deny gains to countries failing to join; prevent countries from "free-riding" (by letting other countries comply but not complying themselves); and remove the incentive for other countries, observing the free riders, to follow suit.[8] The Montreal Protocol commits signatories to ban the import of controlled substances from nonparties, as well as products such as refrigerators containing CFCs. It also calls for consideration of the feasibility of a process ban, affecting such production methods as computer chips manufactured using CFCs as a cleaning solvent.

As noted in chapter 2, numerous issues confront efforts to intermesh these obligations with other obligations under GATT.

First is the question of *parties* and *nonparties*: If some countries belong to the GATT but have not signed the Montreal Protocol, what rights and obligations do they and other countries have to refrain from trade in ozone-depleting chemicals, and what trade burdens are they justified in bearing in the name of the global commons? Second, how great should the reach of these burdens be? That is, what trade-restricting actions that affect other nations is a party to the Montreal Protocol justified in taking? These issues, which also arise in the tuna-dolphin dispute, are here invoked to enforce not a national law, such as the MMPA, but an international environmental agreement affecting the global commons. Third, the legal standing of an agreement such as the Montreal Protocol has been raised in relation to GATT obligations. Although the Protocol is "later in time" than the GATT articles, if countries are not parties to it, then they have not consented to be bound by it. Finally, because of these complexities, some legal experts suggest that agreements such as the Montreal Protocol should be subjected to a waiver from GATT rules, although critics observe that such a waiver may resolve fewer problems than it creates, as noted in chapter 2.

In response to this troubling state of affairs, the Office of Technology Assessment has suggested several factors that can be helpful in determining whether the trade burdens imposed by international environmental agreements are crucial to their effective functioning, or whether alternative measures more directly aimed at the target of global environmental protection are preferable.[9]

First, the conduct at issue (here the manufacture of products or processes involving ozone-depleting chemicals) should be one with global environmental effects. Such a global externality makes the actions of nonparties especially relevant. In effect, even nonparties to the agreement will affect, and be affected by, the joint conduct of those who deplete the ozone layer. Second, trade burdens imposed in the name of global environmental protection should be matched by corresponding restrictions on the conduct of nations that are parties to the environmental agreement. This consistency is necessary in order to avoid the free rider problem, in which parties employ a "do as I say, not as I do" rule. Third, the number of parties should be sufficiently large that a presumption of wide multilateral participation exists. Of course, this begs the question of the early stages, in which participation may not be large; in the case of the Montreal Protocol, with seventy-nine members in 1992, it was precisely to *induce* participation that certain trade-restricting measures were made part of the agreement. Fourth, in addition to the "stick" of trade restriction, international environmental agreements can create "carrots" in the form of expanded market access or funds available to new parties seeking to come into compliance. In the case of the Montreal Protocol, a multilateral fund was established to assist developing countries seeking to comply. Fifth, the trade burdens imposed should be closely linked to the conduct at issue. In the case of the Montreal Protocol, the products and processes restricted relate directly to ozone depletion. However, the leverage created for compliance may well be greater if applied to a broader set of products; and this may well lead countries to take trade-restricting actions that are more broadly burdensome yet that are arguably justified in the name of environmental goals. Sixth, it is important to consider the issue of "leverage" more precisely: How crucial are trade restrictions to achieve global environmental goals? This issue of cross-matching is similar to the "primarily aimed at " questions discussed in the U.S.-Canada salmon-herring case. If it can be reasonably shown that less trade-burdensome methods of achieving the environmental targets are feasible, then alternatives to trade measures merit consideration.

An underlying issue in all six of these factors is: What body of individuals or nations is to answer these questions? Are these issues for GATT to decide, or for some other multilateral entity more appropriate for the purpose? And since such an entity does not now exist, what existing institutions provide insights into the competency required? These issues are the subject of chapter 6.

Chapter 6

Implications for Policy

As the twentieth century draws to a close, two global trends are converging. The first, and more powerful, is the increasing integration of the world economy, and the resulting interdependence of domestic and international policies affecting trade in goods and services. This trend, reflected in the successful completion of the Uruguay Round of GATT in December 1993, creates both greater trade frictions and greater opportunities to develop mutually beneficial trading relationships. It also tests the rules of trade developed under the auspices of GATT and regional trading arrangements such as the EU and NAFTA.

The second global trend is the imperative to protect the environment, and the need for national and international policies of environmental preservation to reduce the damages that trade can bring. Despite differences in the emphasis given to environment in the North and the South, environmental issues will doubtless continue to dominate international discussion, including North-South dialogues, in the years ahead, especially given the transformation and diminished security threats posed by East-West relations.

These two trends are now intertwining in complex ways. Despite the many technical issues involved, an important and simple complementarity also exists. In much the same way that international trade rules have evolved in and outside of GATT in response to global economic interdependence, so new international environ-

94

mental rules are evolving in response to global environmental inter-dependence. Out of this evolution an opportunity arises to link the objectives of market integration with environmental protection. Curiously, because the gap between environmental standards in the North and South is so great, it is precisely along the North-South axis that the opportunity for such linkage is also greatest.

In the same way that differences in resource endowments create gains from trade between dissimilar nations, so differences in levels of development and environmental protection can create comple-mentarities built on incentives to exchange market access to the North in return for commitments to raise environmental standards in the South. The grand bargain in the making is to link one of the primary objectives of the Uruguay Round of GATT (more open market access) with the objective of the 1992 Rio Conference (raised levels of environmental protection). This is precisely what the negotiations over an environmental side agreement to NAFTA reflected: a promise of access to the markets of North America in return for a commitment to environmental improvements and en-forcement in Mexico. What the NAFTA experience suggests most clearly, however, is that trade rules alone are inadequate to the task: environmental rules are also required. And where such rules are developed, new institutions will be required to monitor and enforce them, typified by the trilateral CEC.

The purpose of the final part of this study is to draw together the implications of the cases and analyses above for policy changes needed both in the United States and in international institutions affecting trade and the environment. The discussion will be divided into three parts: a review of some of the broad lessons of the cases presented in chapters 3–5, an examination of the institutional gaps in existing policy, especially at the international level, with particu-lar attention to the need for an international environmental institu-tion, and a consideration of the specific role of the United States in the development of new institutions and policies.

LESSONS FROM THE CASES

The experiences of both the EU and NAFTA demonstrate the com-plex environmental impacts of moves toward trade liberalization, and suggest that no universal causal linkages exist from market

integration to environmental problems. In the case of the EU, market integration has often been accompanied by increases in trade
protection vis-à-vis the rest of the world, leading to adverse environmental impacts, such as those in agriculture. At the same time,
European integration and liberalization *within* the EU has led to
adverse scale effects, such as those in the transport sector. At an
institutional level, however, integration has brought home to the EU
the importance of both local and transnational environmental damages, and the need to develop more uniform standards and environmental directives to confront them, emanating from the legislative
process in Brussels. The European Court of Justice has also played a
role in formulating common environmental policies, while protecting the principle of "subsidiarity," in which non–trade-distorting
national standards are respected but trade-distorting standards not
essential to environmental health or safety are struck down. Despite
these achievements, the environmental policies of the EU have not
yet overcome the adverse environmental impacts of its agricultural
policies, nor the economic and trade priorities reflected in such
distortions as the manioc export agreement with Thailand. Many
more years of evolution are likely necessary before these policies
reflect the emerging environmental imperative in the EU.

NAFTA has also struggled with the "subsidiarity" of environmental policies, and the temptation to disregard environmental
problems associated with trade reform. In defense of their own
national policies on trade and environment, both Canada and Mexico were initially wary of the U.S.-led calls for a side agreement that
might preempt national laws. However, successful completion of the
side agreement in August 1993 and approval of the total NAFTA
package now promises a remarkable institutional approach to
transnational externalities. The CEC reflects incentives to develop
transnational institutions, similar to those in the EU, that will be
capable of overseeing environmental policies in all three nations.
The critical question is whether these institutions will be able to
successfully balance independent national policies with the need for
oversight and enforcement. The fact that the new commission is the
centerpiece of the environmental side agreement to NAFTA suggests that institutional authority for environmental impacts of trade
integration is a real possibility, and that a separate instrument of

policy aimed specifically at this target can be created. The broader implications of the need for such authority will be explored in greater detail below.

The tuna-dolphin and salmon-herring cases concerned the use of environmental measures as nontariff trade barriers. The much discussed tuna-dolphin case raises many more issues than it answers. Perhaps the most significant is whether nations can exercise "extrajurisdictional" authority over trade in order to make stronger environmental laws effective. In this case, the United States argued unsuccessfully before GATT that the MMPA requires the use of such measures to be effective. The major impact of the GATT panel's rejection of the U.S. arguments was less to clarify the legal issues surrounding product-process distinctions, or the exceptions for trade-distorting environmental measures granted under GATT article XX, than to bolster claims by environmental critics that GATT is institutionally hostile to environmental protection. As Charnovitz notes:

> In addition to ruling that the MMPA violated international trade rules, the GATT panel implicitly dropped a wide net over decades of environmental treaties and laws protecting everything from deep sea whales to stratospheric ozone. Indeed, the panel seemed to go out of its way to validate the popular caricature of the GATT as an inflexible, myopic, moss-grown institution inherently indifferent, if not downright antagonistic, toward ecological protection.[1]

Compared with the tuna-dolphin case, the U.S.-Canada salmon-herring case provides a much clearer example of how environmental measures can function as disguised barriers to trade, and offers a number of criteria that can assist in deciding whether a trade-distorting measure is primarily aimed at environmental objectives. In this case, the attempt by Canada to invoke the environmental exceptions of GATT article XX was rejected in part because the panel was not convinced that the costly and time-consuming procedures used to count the salmon and herring catch would be employed if the only parties affected were the Canadians themselves. The panel in effect argued that the environmental benefits did not outweigh the costs created by the measure in the form of burdens to trade. It also suggested that the same environmental objectives could be met with alternative measures that were less trade-burdensome.

The final case considered, the Montreal Protocol, represents a general class of international environmental agreements that raise important issues for the world trading system. Since the effectiveness of many such agreements appears to depend in part on the use of trade sanctions to induce compliance by signatories and non-signatories, they pose special challenges to the established order of trade rules under GATT. An additional part of this challenge is that these agreements may attempt to reach beyond products to the manufacturing processes used to produce them. While blanket waivers covering such agreements are a possibility, such waivers do not really address the relative impacts of international environmental versus international trade rules. As environmental agreements proliferate, they tend to underscore the need for an institutional authority that can help develop a balanced approach to trade and environmental policy.

What are the overall lessons of these complex cases? Three stand out. First, as noted in chapter 2, in an ideal world trade targets would be pursued with trade policy instruments, and environmental targets with environmental policy instruments, whenever possible. In real-world cases, in which conflict is unavoidable because trade policies lead to environmental damage, or environmental policies are unsustainable without imposing trade burdens, a more complicated set of issues arises. The experiences of both the EU and NAFTA suggest that when trade policies are associated with environmental damages, a separate and high-level institutional authority operating across national governments (although not necessarily "above" them) is necessary. In the EU, the European Commission and the European Court largely share this authority; in the case of NAFTA, the CEC will play such a role. With NAFTA as a model, it now seems logical to extend such authority from the regional to the multilateral level.

Second, when either national or global environment policies appear to require the imposition of trade burdens, it is evident from the tuna-dolphin and salmon-herring cases, as well as the Montreal Protocol, that the more carefully targeted these policies are to the environmental issue at hand, and the more equalized the trade burdens imposed in the home and foreign markets, the less likely they are to be perceived by the nations affected as unjustified. Here too, however, an institutional conduit is needed through which environmental information and expertise can pass. It is unlikely that GATT, as such, is the appropriate institutional authority for such a task.

Third, in the development of such institutional authority for the environment, it is important to invest it with sufficient power to affect national policies, but not so much as unduly to threaten the sovereign rights of national governments. Here the principle of subsidiarity remains important. If new environmental institutions appear to promise the large bureaucracies associated with many international organizations, and substantial interference with national policies, they are unlikely to be met with great favor. Instead, efforts should be made to "lightly engineer" such institutions. As in building an elegantly constructed but strong bridge, creating an institutional basis for environmental oversight and expertise should strive to carry the weight of upgrading national and international environmental rules with a minimum of materials but a maximum of strength.

Here the historical experience of GATT can be instructive. When GATT was formed in 1947, it was conceived as part of the larger International Trade Organization (ITO), with powers reaching beyond those of the GATT articles. Largely because of fears in the U.S. Congress over a loss of sovereign authority (both to other nations and to the executive branch), the ITO was never approved, and only the enabling articles of GATT survived. It is widely felt that the GATT articles, while remarkably successful in creating a framework for trade reform, were *too* lightly engineered to bear the weight of increasing global trade flows, especially as time elapsed and the number of GATT members grew.[2]

For these reasons, the ITO idea has been reformulated and is now partially contained in the World Trade Organization (WTO) resulting from the successful Uruguay Round. While some in Congress will question the WTO for some of the same reasons that the ITO was viewed suspiciously, a stronger institutional authority backing the GATT articles would probably have proven useful to trade liberalization (and U.S. interests) in the past. As one of the largest trading nations in the world, the United States undoubtedly would have exercised substantial influence and leadership in the

ITO, and will do so in the WTO. Rather than compromising the sovereignty of the United States, such an organization will facilitate the extension of U.S. influence, helping to realize U.S. trading goals and objectives. From a multilateral perspective, the WTO will be better able to bear the weight of the huge volume of global trade, and the conflicts and opportunities such trade represents.

For largely analogous reasons, a World Environmental Organization (WEO) would allow the United States to lead a global effort for environmental improvements. Yet such an organization would also threaten the sovereign authority over environmental issues of some nations—possibly including the United States, and certainly including many developing countries. Hence, light but strong engineering is called for here as well. Rather than being invested with powers over trade, a WEO should work alongside, but separately from, those institutions concerned with trade policy. This is simply the multilateral version of the "targets and instruments" distinction employed above. A WEO would thus work to advance environmental improvements that are coordinated with and linked to increases in market access and expanded trading opportunities under the GATT system. As a first step, an international environmental institution would require a secretariat, like that of GATT, and a definition of purpose and participation. It is here that the discussions in NAFTA over the CEC take on global significance.

TOWARD A WEO

If environmental values are to receive the priority they deserve, international institutions must change. Existing bodies must be reorganized, and new institutions created. While the exact shape and details of these institutions remain in the future, their general character can be delineated—and should be supported by national leadership—now.

Yet to be successful, global environmental institutions should not be monolithic. A WEO should be thought of as a "chapeau," or overarching body, in relation to what will be a highly complex international management structure.[3] Currently hundreds of international environmental agreements—multilateral and bilateral—

and thousands of official, semiofficial, and private groups are responsible for environmental management. While fragmented, these efforts are often effective precisely because they focus on specific issues and problems, and involve local and national participants who have direct links to them. Their role and participation in structuring an overarching institutional approach will be vital.

At the same time, a need exists to give visibility and force to environmental targets and instruments at the international level—to acknowledge this sphere of policymaking as equal to the international trading regime. For these purposes, a multilateral environmental organization takes on the same significance in its own sphere as the WTO resulting from the Uruguay Round.

The side agreement negotiations in NAFTA, which over two years of consultation between government and environmental groups produced the CEC, provide a prototype for the WEO. This prototype is enormously important. What is required is to extend the logic leading to the trilateral CEC to the multilateral level. Some circles already view the CEC as a radical innovation; the extension of its form to the multilateral level would perhaps be considered more radical still. Yet the time for new thinking and a balance of forces between trade and the environment is now.

As an overarching instrument, the WEO would not threaten the existence of more decentralized institutions (including the CEC), but would help give these institutions a legitimacy and force they do not possess. This can be especially important in developing countries, where the "voice" of environmental concerns is often weak. In many ways, the voice a WEO would offer to the environment would be similar to that the International Commission on Human Rights, meeting annually in Geneva, offers to human rights concerns.

Let us pursue the elements of a WEO by thinking first in terms of the trilateral CEC resulting from NAFTA. First, the commission has important oversight responsibilities (if given the resources necessary to fulfill its mandate). Second, it can promote enforcement of national environmental laws, and involve citizens in a more open process of trade and environmental policy formulation. Third, the commission provides for dispute resolution and settlement procedures, and the systematic involvement of environmental and scientific experts. Finally, dedicated sources of funding are established for border environmental infrastructure, cleanup, and conservation programs.

The commitment of most of the major environmental interest groups[4] to NAFTA is built on this new institutional authority, which fills a major gap. For the first time, national governments and major trading nations have acknowledged, through negotiations, the importance of the trade-environment interface, and the need for institutions to balance a perceived lack of attention to the environment.

These discussions are a harbinger of the agenda to which a WEO will need to respond. Justin Ward and Lynn Fischer of the Natural Resources Defense Council have described this agenda as being composed of several elements.[5] First, a WEO must have the capacity to induce nations to upgrade enforcement of environmental laws that may exist on paper, but are not operational in fact. For example, a 1992 General Accounting Office sample of U.S. majority-owned *maquiladora* factories found that none of the six sampled had conducted an environmental impact assessment for new plants established in Mexico, despite such a requirement under the Mexican General Ecology Law of 1988.[6] The capacity to publicize such noncompliance would be an important mechanism for a WEO, even if it lacked enforcement powers of its own.

While the representatives to a WEO would, like GATT representatives, be government officials, opportunities must also exist for citizen and expert involvement. A Multilateral Commission on Environment (MACE) could be established as part of a WEO, composed of a standing group of environmental experts from all member countries, including nongovernmental representatives. Its meetings would be open to the public, and would allow worldwide access to the data and analysis underlying its work. The primary focus of this work would be to propose ways to "harmonize up" national environmental standards, while carefully considering the technical issues and problems of this process for developing countries. MACE would issue regular reports and related documents proposing improved policies, identifying environmental "hot spots," and recommending special projects for national governments. This process would allow for public comments from any group, governmental or nongovernmental. The effect would be to open the WEO to full public participation and review.

Third, a WEO would work closely with the World Bank (IBRD) and other multilateral lending agencies, such as the European Bank for Reconstruction and Development (EBRD) and the Inter-American Bank (BID), as well as the International Monetary Fund (IMF), to develop funding for environmental projects to upgrade national infrastructure, especially for waste water treatment, sanitation, and hazardous waste disposal. National governments could be encouraged to establish an initial tranche of $10 billion for these purposes to operate on a revolving basis through the Global Environment Facility.[7] This funding would focus primarily on projects in developing countries in Latin America, Asia, Africa, and in eastern Europe and the former Soviet Union, where national resources for environmental improvements are most scarce.

Fourth, a WEO and MACE would work jointly with GATT and the Organization for Economic Cooperation and Development (OECD) to identify trade measures that threaten environmental quality, and to develop environmental policies that are least burdensome to trade expansion. In cases in which trade burdens due to environmental policies come before GATT dispute settlement panels, such as the tuna-dolphin and U.S.-Canada salmon-herring cases, MACE would utilize its expertise to offer evidence, analysis, and proposed alternatives to the policies in dispute.

The organization of the institution will be important. While a highly elaborated plan will require a great deal of analysis and consultation, some basic questions can be addressed now. As a first principle, it is well to ask whether such an organization is really needed, in light of the UNEP and related work by development agencies such as the United Nations Development Programme and the Commission on Sustainable Development created as a result of the 1992 Rio Conference. While supplementing and drawing on the work of these groups, knowledgeable observers and participants still support a WEO.[8]

Elliot L. Richardson, former U.S. representative to the Law of the Sea Conference and U.S. secretary of defense, argues forcefully (in the specific context of climate change) for a permanent multilateral body, whether a "beefed-up UNEP" or an entity patterned on GATT itself, and notes that "it may not make a crucial difference whether an old agency is given new duties or a new one is brought into existence."[9] If one extends this argument beyond the issue of climate change (to which it was addressed), the WEO and its commission would then have a role in carrying out the tasks outlined above—specifically, focusing on defining targets for upgrading national environmental policies and standards; reporting on progress toward the achievement of these targets; monitoring and verifying national performance; coordinating technical environmental assistance with multilateral lending agencies; and providing additional evidence and expertise in the context of trade-environment issues in GATT, in the OECD, and in cooperation with national governments and nongovernmental organizations.[10] Here it could help, and be helped by, many more decentralized groups. As Richardson notes:

> The skillful use of these devices would create substantial incentives for member states to improve their environmental performance. Nongovernmental organizations would be watching, exhorting and pushing. Domestic awareness of the national effort would be heightened by the international attention it attracted. Media coverage would be correspondingly intensified. The attention thereby focused on the government's response would generate pressure to raise its level. It is arguable, indeed, that the self-reinforcing process thus set in motion could become a formidable substitute for official action—more effective than regulation and far less expensive than its enforcement. If this happens, what has generally been called "soft law" will become progressively harder.[11]

The linking of the environmental activities of a WEO to market access and trade reform in GATT, the OECD, and the multilateral lending agencies, will create additional incentives to comply and "get aboard." Especially through the linking of market access goals and environmental improvements, incentives in the North and South can be brought into closer accord. Lawrence Susskind and Connie Ozawa of the Massachusetts Institute of Technology have noted that "environmental negotiations, up to now, have been conducted largely in isolation from negotiations on other international issues such as debt, trade, or security." Linking these issues enhances the potential for mutual gains, since "the goal of a well-structured negotiation is not to encourage compromise but to find ways of ensuring that all parties will be better off if they cooperate."[12]

The way in which membership in a WEO and its commission is structured will also be important. As noted, the WEO will require the contracting parties to be national governments with official delegations. It would serve as a general "chapeau" for the growing number of international environmental agreements, such as the Montreal Protocol, just as GATT serves as an umbrella over a large number of special trading agreements and arrangements. It would have its own small secretariat. MACE, as a multilateral commission, would be more open, and should include representatives from not only governments but businesses, environmental groups, and other interested nongovernmental organizations.[13] The general structure of such an organization is shown in Figure 3.[14]

Finally, questions remain over whether GATT itself requires major institutional changes to accommodate a "green agenda." It is our view that GATT is not an environmental organization, and should not become one. However, if the GATT charter were expanded to allow for a sufficiently well-engineered WEO and MACE, much pressure to "reform GATT" would be diverted constructively into the development of instruments directly aimed at environmental targets. The environmental community will demand, with reason, that global environmental institutions not be subservient to GATT. Long before these environmental institutions are fully developed, however, GATT itself must adapt to a balanced relationship between trade and the environment. As the highly respected trade expert Geza Feketekuty has noted, "There is wide agreement among GATT members that the GATT's trade rules need to be adapted to better support the achievement of environmental goals at both the national and global level."[15] Among these changes, the exceptions for the conservation of natural resources falling under GATT article XX should be interpreted to allow as acceptable all environmental measures undertaken by national governments that are primarily aimed at environmental objectives, in some cases including extra-jurisdictional measures necessary to make environmental protection effective. This would include the trade restrictions implicit in agreements such as the Montreal Protocol.[16] Such measures might be subject to a waiver, in effect until a WEO and MACE were in

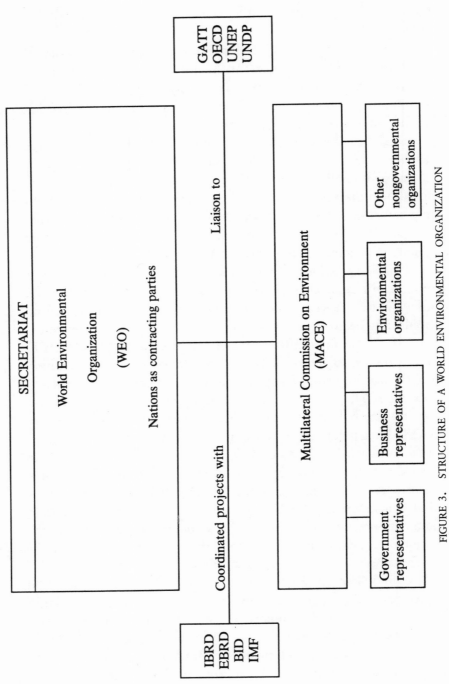

FIGURE 3. STRUCTURE OF A WORLD ENVIRONMENTAL ORGANIZATION

place, creating additional incentives in the trade community to move the WEO to the top of the agenda. Once the WEO and MACE were in place, the waiver would automatically end, and the WEO and MACE would take on the collaborative role with GATT and the other multilateral institutions outlined above.

THE RESPONSIBILITIES OF THE UNITED STATES

In the trade-environment debate, as in many other global issues, the United States must lead. For more than a decade, the United States relinquished its role as a leader in international environmental affairs, while continuing aggressively to pursue both regional and multilateral trade agreements. The consequence was to open it to criticism that it was pursuing freer trade without regard to the environmental consequences. Restoring balance in the relationship between free trade and a protected environment now requires that comparable efforts be undertaken to create new rules for international environmental policy. In many respects, the opportunity to take the lead in this arena fits naturally with the redefinition of international security resulting from the end of the Cold War.[17]

Both trade and the environment have emerged in the post–Cold War era as issues of overwhelming importance, because human salvation is increasingly defined in economic and ecological terms. Until recently, ecological security was often regarded as competitive with economic prosperity, creating an either/or proposition for policymakers. While trade-offs will often be necessary between environmental quality and unrestrained trade, it is increasingly clear that many areas of complementarity exist as well.[18] We have argued that to exploit this complementarity, it will be necessary to develop rules and incentives for environmental protection at both national and international levels that accomplish their objectives with as few burdens for market forces as is feasible; likewise, market expansion must proceed within constraints that protect nations from the negative environmental impacts of economic activity, whether these impacts are felt locally, transnationally, or globally.

The reason that the United States must take the lead in promoting and exploiting this complementarity is its prominence in both the economic and the environmental arenas. Despite progress in the EU on both economic and environmental grounds, the unified Europe and new European leadership promoted early in the decade have not emerged.[19] Japan, clearly a powerful force in trade, and a leader in some areas of environmental control technologies, has only recently begun to embrace the Uruguay Round goals of market access and the Rio Conference objective of global environmental improvement.[20] By contrast, NAFTA offers in microcosm precisely the sort of complementarity between trade liberalization and environmental protection possible on a global scale: a grand bargain between North and South on trade and the environment.

NAFTA points the way to three elements necessary if the United States is to create the conditions for a balanced trade and environmental regime at the global level. The first of these is a domestic commitment to upgrade and enforce U.S. environmental standards and to promote similar standards for U.S. companies operating abroad (in countries such as Mexico), setting a clear example for the rest of the world. The second element is to negotiate a compact with the other industrialized economies of the North (such as Canada) to pursue general trade-environment linkages by creating a WEO and MACE, generalizing the concept of the CEC. The third element is the negotiation of a corresponding compact with the countries of the South (such as Mexico) in which market access is granted in return for commitments to upgrade and enforce environmental standards.

Together, these three elements constitute a multilateral agenda for U.S. action. It is fortunate that they also coincide with many of the expressed priorities of the Clinton administration, including aggressive implementation and enforcement of domestic environmental protection, global leadership in consummating the Uruguay Round, and the desire to promote North-South bargains linking market access and environmental improvements through agreements such as NAFTA. Vice President Gore, in his own analysis of environmental issues, is especially supportive of the potential complementarity between economic opportunity and environmental improvement.[21] By extending this view into international policymaking, the current administration can leave a permanent mark on the institutional landscape with a WEO and MACE.

The appropriate venue for creating such international institutions is likely to be a joint forum following on the Uruguay Round and the 1992 Rio Conference. In addition to constituting the MEO and MACE, these follow-on discussions would focus on all three of the issues that have occupied this study: the environmental impacts of trade; the trade impacts of environmental regulation; and the interactions between multilateral trade and environmental obligations. This would be more than simply a "green round" of GATT; it would be the beginning of new global rules for the environment.

Achieving a new balance between trade and environmental interests is likely to be the most lasting set of issues and challenges for this and future governments, both North and South. In contrast to the balance of destructive forces that has dominated the postwar era, this new balance is one of humanitarian gains—both economic and environmental. To achieve such gains would be to reward the welfare of this generation, and generations to come, with continued prosperity and improved environmental quality.

Appendix A

THE WELFARE ANALYTICS OF
TRADE AND ENVIRONMENTAL POLICY[1]

Kym Anderson presents a simple analytical description of trade and environmental policy interaction that clarifies many issues, as well as underscoring how difficult they are to resolve. He first describes a small country facing both market failures and the prospect of trade liberalization, in which the country's own actions do not affect the rest of the world. He then considers a large country, whose actions do have global effects.[2]

Suppose a small country produces or consumes a commodity, such as corn, and an externality results from the market's failure to reflect the impact of its (and only its) production or consumption on the natural environment. An example of a production externality might be soil erosion that reduces the productivity of agricultural lands and lowers water quality. An example of a consumption externality might be water pollution from farm chemicals that raises the risk of water-borne disease.[3]

The result of the externality is to drive a "wedge" between marginal private and social costs of production, reflected in the divergence of S and S' in Figure A-1. The demand curve, D, represents marginal private benefits. The price axis refers to the price of

FIGURE A-1. EFFECTS OF OPENING UP A SMALL ECONOMY TO TRADE
IN A PRODUCT WHOSE PRODUCTION IS POLLUTING

(a) Importable

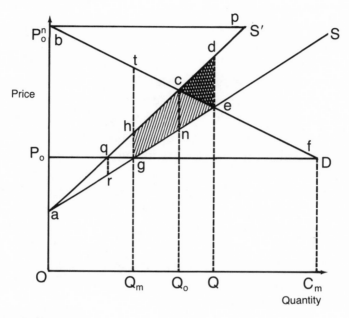

(b) Exportable

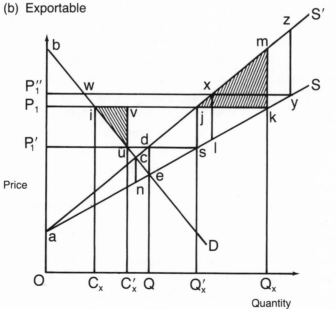

Source: Kym Anderson, "The Standard Welfare Economics of Policies Affecting Trade and the Environment," in Kym Anderson and Richard Blackhurst, eds., *The Greening of World Trade Issues* (Ann Arbor, Mich.: University of Michigan Press, 1992), p. 28.

corn relative to all other prices in the economy, which remain constant throughout.

In this case, OQ is the level of corn production without either international trade or measures to "internalize" environmental impacts such as erosion. Production occurs at point e, the intersection of private marginal benefits and costs. Net social welfare is given as the sum of producer and consumer surplus,[4] minus the social costs of the external effect, or $abe - ade$. Now assume that the country shifts from autarchy (no trade) to open trade. If OP_0 is the prevailing international (border) price, as in Figure A-1(a), production would fall to OQ_m, consumption would rise to OC_m, and Q_mC_m units of corn would be imported. Net social welfare is now $abfg - ahg$, and the welfare gain is $defgh$. This gain from trade is both positive and greater than it would have been if no externality had existed in the form of erosion, represented by the shaded area $degh$. In effect, the country benefits because it imports corn more cheaply than it can produce it, and benefits by reducing soil erosion as well. Imports are "substitutes" for erosion.

On the other hand, suppose OP_1 is the prevailing international (border) price, as in Figure A-1(b). The country would thus become a net exporter of C_xQ_x units of corn if it moved to open trade. Net social welfare would be $abik - amk$, so the welfare effect of trade liberalization without any action to internalize the effects of erosion would be $eik - edmk$, which could be a net gain or net loss, depending on the relative magnitude of the *gain* from trade versus the *loss* from increased erosion as production expanded from Q to Q_x.

From Anderson's analysis, several propositions follow. The first is that liberalizing trade in a good with adverse environmental impacts that are left uncontrolled improves a small country's welfare if it imports the good following liberalization; but if it exports the good, the negative environmental effects are subtracted from the gains from trade, and the welfare effect is ambiguous. By importing the polluting good, a country lets some other country worry about its polluting properties. By exporting it, the country continues to face the social cost of these externalities in the home market.

Now suppose that instead of leaving erosion uncontrolled, the small country combined trade reform with an environmental policy intervention sufficient to internalize the externality. Such an intervention could take the form of a tax, charge, or equivalent regulation or change in property rights.[5] Given such an environmental policy intervention, the gain from trade liberalization is *qcf* in Figure A-1(a) and *cij* in Figure A-1(b), depending on whether corn is imported or exported. In contrast to the situation in which no environmental intervention occurs, this is a net gain in either the importing or the exporting case.

It is important to note, however, that without environmental intervention, the benefits of liberalization for the exporter would be even greater, by *cde*. Hence, an incentive exists for net exporters to forgo environmental interventions because the benefits from trade are reduced somewhat by the production declines resulting from such environmental policy interventions. In this restricted sense, it is accurate to say that environmental interventions reduce an exporting nation's "competitiveness." But the larger loss is in net welfare, in that without such interventions, it is not clear that expanded exports will improve net welfare at all.

However, whether a small country is an importer or an exporter, trade yields welfare gains, provided that a targeted (nearly optimal) environmental policy is introduced.

A third proposition of direct relevance to agricultural trade concerns the relative efficacy of trade and environmental policy instruments. Suppose that instead of targeted environmental policy interventions aimed at erosion control, a trade instrument such as an export tax aimed at the same target was proposed. This is shown in Figure A-1(b). An export tax equal to *js* could be used to lower the price that producers receive from P_1 to P'_1, reducing production and lowering exports from $C_x Q_x$ to $C'_x Q'_x$. This would lower the marginal cost of production to a level equivalent to an environmental intervention, producing a welfare gain of shaded area *jmk*. But the export tax causes consumers to pay $P'_1 P_1$ below the opportunity cost of OP_1, leading to a deadweight welfare loss due to excess domestic consumption $C_x C'_x$, equal to the shaded area *iuv*. Hence, using a trade policy instrument reduces environmental degradation as much as an environmental tax set at the same rate, but at higher cost.[6]

Trade instruments can be used to reduce environmental degradation by a given amount, but they generally will improve welfare less than a more direct intervention at the source of the environmental pollution, and may even worsen welfare.

Moving from the small to the large country case, it is possible that liberalization or environmental policies will affect world prices, so that the price lines in Figure A-1 are no longer horizontal. Moreover, the environmental policies and polluting activities of large countries such as the United States or the EU will have global impacts, spilling over and ultimately back into home markets and welfare. Finally, policy changes in large countries may have demonstration or leadership effects on other countries.

In summary, the welfare effects of liberalizing trade are ambiguous if environmental externalities are left uncontrolled; but if they are largely internalized by an appropriately targeted environmental policy, the joint "liberalization effect" and "environmental effect" on welfare is positive.

Simple welfare analysis thus offers an analytical foundation for issues in trade and the environment. At an empirical level, however, there is still very little understanding of the effects of trade liberalization on the environment, and how different commodities and countries will be affected. Trade liberalization is also unlikely to be total or all-inclusive, so that distortions and adverse environmental impacts will remain.

Appendix B

SUMMARY OF MEETINGS:
TRADE AND THE ENVIRONMENT STUDY GROUP

Codirectors C. Michael Aho, director of Economic Studies at the Council on Foreign Relations, and C. Ford Runge, professor of agricultural and applied economics at the University of Minnesota, organized eight meetings as part of the year-long study on the interrelation between international trade and the environment.

Participants in the study group were drawn from academia, government, private nongovernmental organizations, and business to ensure a well-balanced discussion. Special invitations were extended to a variety of environmental and church groups, including grass-roots groups located outside of Washington. Ambassador Michael B. Smith, of SJS Advanced Strategies, chaired all meetings. Five of the eight sessions were held at the Council on Foreign Relations in New York City; the remaining three took place in Minneapolis, Austin, and Seattle.

The first meeting, on June 9, 1992, outlined the three central issues the group would be exploring in depth over the next year: the impact of trade liberalization on environmental quality; the potential use of environmental measures as nontariff trade barriers; and the relationship between multilateral environmental agreements and trade obligations under GATT. The speakers at the first meeting were Marcia Aronoff and Peter Emerson, both of the Environmental Defense Fund; Robert Weissler of the Office of Technology Assessment; and Robert Housman of the Center for International Environmental Law.

The second meeting, on July 8, 1992, examined the impact of trade liberalization on environmental quality and explored the relationship between economic activity and the concept of sustainable development. The speakers were Stewart Hudson of the National Wildlife Federation; Justin Ward of the Natural Resources Defense Council; and Gene Grossman of Princeton University.

The third meeting, on September 14, 1992, addressed the way in which environmental standards can act as nontariff trade barriers. The speakers were Konrad von Moltke of Dartmouth College, who discussed trends in environmental regulation and the move to a more preventive approach to environmental management; and Robert Hudec of the University of Minnesota Law School, who spoke on various legal tests that could be used to determine when domestic environmental measures could be regarded as unjustifiable restrictions on trade.

At the next meeting, on October 21, 1992, the speakers were Eli Whitney Debevoise II of Arnold & Porter; Daniel Esty of the Environmental Protection Agency; and John Whalley of the University of Western Ontario. The discussion concerned the relationship between multilateral environmental agreements and trade obligations (such as nondiscrimination under GATT) and examined, in detail, the tuna-dolphin debate.

The first regional meeting was held in Minneapolis, on December 9, 1992. This session concentrated on the impact on the Midwest of the trade-environment debate. The speakers, who focused on high-technology and agricultural issues, were Michael Bonsignore, chief executive officer of the Honeywell Corporation; Lee Berlin of LecTec Co., a medical products company; C. Ford Runge of the University of Minnesota; and Annette Higby of the Center for Rural Affairs in Nebraska.

The second regional session was held in Austin, on January 14, 1993. This meeting focused on NAFTA, environmental problems along the U.S.-Mexican border, and institutional arrangements for an environmental commission and North American trade commission. The speakers were Sidney Weintraub of the LBJ School of Public Affairs at the University of Texas; Ray Mikesell of the University of Oregon; Jan Gilbreath Rich of the University of Texas; Gary Williams of Texas A&M University; and Peter Emerson of the Environmental Defense Fund.

At the third regional meeting, in Seattle, on March 4, 1993, the discussion focused on trade and environmental issues central to the Northwest: the fisheries and timber industries. Stanley Barer, a partner at Garvey, Schubert & Barer, and Mike Fitzgerald, from the Washington State Department of Trade and Economic Development, presented a profile of the region's economic, political, and environmental qualities. Then the following speakers addressed the concerns of conservationists, commercial and recreational fisheries, and state regulatory agencies: Lorrie Bodi of American Rivers National Conservation Group; Prudence Fox of the National Marine Fisheries Service; and Wally Pereyra of Profish, Inc. Other speakers addressed the conflicts and issues of concern in the timber industry: Lynn Endicott of Weyerhaeuser Company; Bruce Lippke of the Center for International Trade in Forest Products; Richard Nafziger of the Washington State Office of the Insurance Commissioner; and Melanie Rowland of the Institute for Environmental Studies at the University of Washington.

The final session of the study group was held at the Council on Foreign Relations in New York City on May 6, 1993. This meeting examined institutional innovation and reform within the trade-environment debate. Three speakers addressed various aspects of this topic. Steve Charnovitz of the Competitiveness Policy Council spoke on the scope of GATT article XX in allowing exceptions to GATT rules for international environmental agreements. Justin Ward, of the Natural Resources Defense Council, and Stephen Mumme, of Colorado State University, spoke of the concerns surrounding the role and definition of a North American Commission on Environmental Cooperation and the possibility of an international environmental organization and its relationship to GATT.

Appendix C

TRADE AND THE ENVIRONMENT STUDY GROUP

Composite Roster

Chairman: Michael B. Smith—SJS Advanced Strategies

Codirectors: C. Michael Aho—Council on Foreign Relations

            C. Ford Runge—University of Minnesota

John Adams—University of Minnesota

Nancy Alderman—Environmental Defense Fund

Olof Allgardh—Winthrop, Stimson, Putnam & Roberts

Marcia Aronoff—Environmental Defense Fund

John Audley—Sierra Club

Ken Berlin—Winthrop, Stimson, Putnam & Roberts

Jagdish Bhagwati—Columbia University

Michael Bonsignore—Honeywell

William Branson—Princeton University

Daniel Brinza—Office of the U.S. Trade Representative

Robin Broad—American University

Jeffrey Broadbent—University of Minnesota

Janet Welsh Brown—World Resources Institute

Sabrina Burgi—Council on Foreign Relations

Robert Cattanah—Oppenheimer, Wolf & Donnelly

Steve Charnovitz—Competitiveness Policy Council
Aimee Cotton—Council on Foreign Relations
Wilfredo Cruz—World Bank
Juan Antonio Cuellar—Instituto para la Proteccion Ambiental de
    Nuevo Leon, Mexico
Nomsa Daniels—New School for Social Research
Elizabeth Danon—Consulate of Mexico, Austin
Kristin Dawkins—Institute for Agriculture and Trade Policy
Eli Whitney Debevoise II—Arnold & Porter
William Diebold, Jr.—Council on Foreign Relations
Peter Emerson—Environmental Defense Fund
Daniel Esty—U.S. Environmental Protection Agency
Daniel Farber—University of Minnesota
Lynn Fischer—Natural Resources Defense Council
Michael Fitzgerald—Forward Washington
Greg Forge—Waste Management, Inc.
Dean Freudenberger—Luther-Northwestern Theological Seminary
Robert Froehlke—IDS Mutual Fund Group
Sanford Gaines—Office of the U.S. Trade Representative
Daniel Gifford—University of Minnesota
Heidi Gifford—Council on Foreign Relations
Joseph Greenwald—Consultant
Gene Grossman—Princeton University
Luis Manuel Guerra—Inaine
Michael Harper—University of Minnesota
Milda Hedblom—Augsburg College
Annette Higby—Center for Rural Affairs
Michael Hodin—Pfizer International, Inc.
Ann Hollick—U.S. State Department
Robert Holt—University of Minnesota
Gary Horlick—O'Melveny & Myers
James Houck—University of Minnesota
Robert Housman—Center for International Environmental Law
Edward Hoyt—U.S. Council for International Business
Mont Hoyt—Verner, Liipfert, Bernhard, McPherson and Hand,
    Chartered
Robert Hudec—University of Minnesota
Stewart Hudson—National Wildlife Federation

Sol Hurwitz—Committee for Economic Development
Eveyln Iritani—*Seattle Post Intelligencer*
John Jackson—University of Michigan
Patricia Jacobs—Market Strategies International
Robbin Johnson—Cargill Inc.
Patrick Jones—Washington Public Ports Association
Geri Joseph—University of Minnesota
Robert Kapp—Washington Council on International Trade
Abraham Katz—U.S. Council for International Business
Michele Kay—*Austin American-Statesman*
Kenneth Keller—Council on Foreign Relations
Mary Kelly—Texas Center for Policy Studies
Randall Kindley—University of Minnesota
Ronald Kramer—U.S. Department of Commerce
Ronald Kroese—Land Stewardship Project
Marshall Kuykendall—Texas Department of Commerce
Jeffrey Lang—Winthrop, Stimson, Putnam & Roberts
Tahirih Lee—University of Minnesota
Marc Levinson—*Newsweek*
Patrick Low—World Bank
Christopher Makins—Aspen Institute
Andrew Mangan—Texas General Land Office
Katharine Mardirosian—Council on Foreign Relations
James McIntire—University of Washington
Ray Mikesell—University of Oregon
Fred Morrison—University of Minnesota
Kim Munholland—University of Minnesota
Michael Northrop—Rockefeller Brothers Fund
Seamus O'Cleireacain—Ford Foundation
Santiago Onate—Procurador Federal de Proteccion al Ambiente, Mexico
François Ortalo-Magné—University of Minnesota
Sylvia Ostry—University of Toronto
Teofilo Ozuna—Texas A&M University
Robert Paarlberg—Wellesley College
Mechel Paggi—American Farm Bureau Federation
Charles Pearson—Johns Hopkins University
Gareth Porter—Environmental and Energy Study Institute

Philip Potter—Charles Walker Associates
Rodrigo Prudencio—National Wildlife Federation
Oscar Ramirez—U.S. Environmental Protection Agency
Philip Raup—University of Minnesota
Don Reeves—Bread for the World
Robert Reinstein—U.S. State Department
Mark Reis—Port of Seattle
Richard Remnek—Kemper Securities, Inc.
Jan Gilbreath Rich—University of Texas
Ronald Roskens—U.S. Agency for International Development
Vernon Ruttan—University of Minnesota
Chris Schlect—Northwest Horticultural Council
Anya Schoolman—U.S. Environmental Protection Agency
Jack Sheehan—United Steelworkers of America
Philip Sherwood—Sherwood & McKenzie
William Sippel—Doherty, Rumble & Butler
Murray Smith—Carleton University
Amy Solomon—Northwest Renewable Resources Center
Paul Sommers—Northwest Policy Center
Mike Soto—Attorney General of Texas
Bruce Stokes—*National Journal*
Roger Stone—Council on Foreign Relations
Lawrence Summers—World Bank
Carmen Suro-Bredie—Office of the U.S. Trade Representative
Mary Tacheny—Minnesota Catholic Conference
Eleanor Tejirian—American Assembly
Gerald Torres—University of Minnesota
Jesse Trevino—Attorney General of Texas
Ann Tutweiler—Central Soya
Al Utton—University of New Mexico
Nester Valencia—El Paso Community Foundation
Philip Vande Kamp—University of Minnesota
James Vesely—*The Seattle Times*
Alison von Klemperer—Council on Foreign Relations
Konrad von Moltke—Dartmouth College
Justin Ward—Natural Resources Defense Council
Robert Warrick—Sierra Club
Michael Weinstein—*The New York Times*

Sidney Weintraub—University of Texas
Timothy Weiskel—John F. Kennedy School of Government
Robert Weissler—U.S. Office of Technology Assessment
Delane Welsch—University of Minnesota
John Whalley—University of Western Ontario
Jennifer Whitaker—Council on Foreign Relations
Gary Williams—Texas A&M University
Larry Williams—Sierra Club
S. Linn Williams—Gibson, Dunn & Crutcher
Irving Williamson—Port Authority of New York and New Jersey
Edith Wilson—Burson Marsteller
Joseph Wolf—NSP Co.

Notes

CHAPTER 1

1. All quotations are from the *New York Times* ad of December 14, 1992, p. A12, which reproduced with minor changes a version of April 20, 1992.
2. Mark Silbergeld, *Point by Point Analysis of the Text* (Washington, D.C.: Consumers Union, 1992).

CHAPTER 2

1. Douglas Southgate and Meri Whitaker, "Promoting Resource Degradation in Latin America: Tropical Deforestation, Soil Erosion, and Coastal Ecosystem Disturbance in Ecuador," *Economic Development and Cultural Change*, vol. 40, no. 4 (July 1992), pp. 787–807; and E. B. Barbier, B. A. Aylward, J. C. Burgess, and J. T. Bishop, "Environmental Effects of Trade in the Forestry Sector." (Prepared for the Joint Session of Trade and Environment Experts, OECD, Paris. London Environmental Economics Centre, International Institute for Environment and Development, London, October 28, 1991).
2. Tim T. Phipps, Pierre R. Crosson, and Kent A. Price, "Agriculture and the Environment" (Washington, D.C.: Resources for the Future, National Center for Food and Agricultural Policy, 1986).
3. Richard N. L. Andrews, *Environmental Policy and Administrative Change: Implementation of the National Environmental Policy Act* (Lexington, Mass.: Lexington Books, 1977).
4. Keith Bradsher, "U.S. Appeals Trade-Accord Requirement," *New York Times*, August 25, 1993, p. C1.
5. Under regulations adopted by the Council on Environmental Quality, a more rapid "legislative EIS" has been used in connection with numerous interna-

123

tional agreements, including the Montreal Protocol in 1987 and the Compact of Free Association, affecting Palau, the Marshall Islands, and the Federated States of Micronesia, in 1984. See "Brief of *Amici Curiae* Natural Resources Defense Council, et al.," U.S. Court of Appeals for the District of Columbia Circuit, No. 93-5212, *Public Citizen, et al. v. U.S. Trade Representative*, August 14, 1993.

6. Jan Gilbreath Rich, *Planning the Border's Future: The Mexican-U.S. Integrated Border Environmental Plan* (Austin: U.S.-Mexican Policy Studies Program, Lyndon B. Johnson School of Public Affairs, The University of Texas, 1992).

7. See GATT article III:4 on national treatment; article XX for exceptions for conservation, public health, etc., and GATT article III and GATT Standards Code article 2.1 on "unnecessary obstacles to international trade." These issues are distinguishable from two related questions: whether foreign governments have inadequate environmental protection laws; and whether such lower levels of regulation create an uneven playing field for competing domestic industries. In the first case, the harm resulting from inadequate protection is degradation of the global environment. If *trade* sanctions are proposed in response, then a problem arises insofar as governments attempt to reach beyond their own territory to punish foreign industries. A rejection of this "extrajurisdictionality" was a basis for the controversial tuna-dolphin decision of a GATT panel in 1991, discussed in detail in chapter 4. In the second case, the uneven playing field resulting from lower regulatory oversight, especially in developing countries, may create a competitive disadvantage for industries in countries where oversight is higher. In effect, the low regulatory environment can be seen as a form of subsidy. Trade remedies have been proposed, including a countervailing duty to "even" the burden, or export bans on affected products, such as timber. The problem in terms of GATT law involves how broadly to define a subsidy, as well as the abrogation of responsibility for tariffs bound by previous agreements and prohibitions against quantitative restrictions.

8. See Robert Hudec and Daniel Farber, "Distinguishing Environmental Measures from Trade Barriers." (Prepared for Workshop on International Economic Policy, University of Minnesota, November 17, 1992.) The discussion that follows is based largely on this workshop presentation.

9. *International Trade Reporter*, May 27, 1992 (*Mississippi Poultry Association Inc. v. Madigan*, No. J91-0086[W], DC SMiss 4/23/92).

10. See Walter Russell Mead, "Bushism, Found," *Harpers Magazine*, vol. 285 (September 1992), pp. 34–45.

11. This test is provided in GATT articles XX(a), (b), and (d). These general exceptions allow measures to be undertaken for domestic reasons even if they impose burdens on trade. Under article XX(b), for example, measures must be "necessary to protect human, animal or plant life or health." Articles XX(a) and XX(d) refer, respectively, to "public morals" and securing compliance with custom laws, state monopolies, patents, and trademarks.

12. Robert Hudec, personal communication, September 14, 1992.

13. This test is related to the exception under GATT article XX(g) "relating to the conservation of exhaustible natural resources," if such measures are accompanied by similar domestic restrictions on production or consumption.

14. The Standards Code contained prohibitions against "unnecessary obstacles to international trade," elaborated in the Uruguay Round negotiations in a new draft on technical barriers to trade. The draft text (article 2.2) invokes the logic of "necessity," stating: "Parties shall ensure that technical regulations are not prepared, adopted or applied with a view to or with the effect of creating unnecessary obstacles to international trade. For this purpose, technical regulations shall not be more trade-restrictive than necessary to fulfill a legitimate objective, taking account of the risks non-fulfillment would create."

Then, in a footnote, the rationale of proportionality is stated: "*This provision is intended to ensure proportionality between regulations and the risks non-fulfillment of legitimate objectives would create.*" Such legitimate objectives are, among others, national security, protection of human health and safety, animal or plant life or health, and the environment. Assessments of such risks are to take into account available scientific information and technological possibilities, as well as the end use of the product.

15. This test arises from the preamble to GATT article XX: a measure may not be applied in a way that is a "disguised restriction on international trade." This language also appears in the draft text on sanitary and phytosanitary measures, part of the Uruguay Round agriculture negotiations.

16. For an excellent overview, see David A. Wirth, "A Matchmaker's Challenge: Marrying International Law and American Environmental law," *Virginia Journal of International law*, vol. 32, no. 2 (Winter 1992), pp. 377–420. I am also indebted to Robert Housman for his clear presentation of these issues at various meetings of the Council on Foreign Relations Study Group on Trade and the Environment.

17. The Montreal Protocol on Substances that Deplete the Ozone Layer, *adopted and opened for signature* September 16, 1987, reprinted in I.L.M. vol. 26, p. 1541 (1987) (entered into force January 1, 1989). See U.S. Congress, Office of Technology Assessment (OTA), *Trade and Environment: Conflicts and Opportunities* (Washington, D.C.: U.S. Government Printing Office, 1992), ch. 3, pp. 42–46.

18. Vienna Convention on the Law of Treasures, opened for signature May 23, 1969, UN Doc. A/COIF. 39/27, I.L.M. vol. 8, p. 679, Article 30, I.L.M. vol. 8, p. 691. For a general discussion, see Robert F. Housman and D. Zaelke, "Trade, Environment and Sustainable Development: A Primer" *Hastings International and Comparative Law Review*, vol. 15 (Summer 1992), pp. 535–612.

19. Housman notes that "this approach may be broader than actually necessary to insulate the environmental objectives desired. Further, by imperiling free trade this approach may lead to a weakening of the environmental agreements in question." See Robert Housman, *The Interaction of International Trade and Environmental Agreements* (Washington, D.C.: Center for International Environmental Law, 1992), p. 3.

20. See John Jackson, "World Trade Rules and Environmental Policies: Congruence or Conflict?" *Washington and Lee Law Review*, vol. 49, no. 4 (Fall 1992), pp. 1227–1278. In this overview of trade and environmental issues, Jackson suggests that even if not customary law, the "weight" of a large number of countries agreeing to an international environmental agreement may affect the

likelihood of a GATT complaint by nonparties (p. 1274). "Sometimes," he writes, "a sufficiently large number of important trading countries have accepted a later treaty such that those members have felt that the risk of complaint by GATT Contracting Parties who have not accepted the later treaty making is minimal. This is legally a bit messy, but may be pragmatically acceptable."

21. See the GATT panel report on "U.S.-Restrictions on Imports of Tuna," September 3, 1991, GATT doc. no. DS21/R, reprinted in I.L.M. vol. 30 (1991), p. 1594. Submitted to GATT member countries on September 3, 1991, made public September 16, 1991. For a critical analysis of the tuna-dolphin panel report, which argues that article XX(g) *should* apply to international environmental agreements, and that the "necessary" test applied by the panel was flawed, see Jeffrey L. Dunoff, "Reconciling International Trade with Preservation of the Global Commons: Can We Prosper and Protect?" *Washington and Lee Law Review*, vol. 49, no. 4 (Fall 1992), pp. 1407–1454. Taking a slightly different line of argument, but equally critical of the GATT panel in the tuna-dolphin case, is Steve Charnovitz, "GATT and the Environment: Examining the Issues," *International Environmental Affairs*, vol. 4, no. 3 (Summer 1992), pp. 203–233.

22. Such a waiver would fall under GATT article XXV, para. 5, if two-thirds of the votes cast by a majority of the total GATT membership (a "supermajority") approved it. Although such a waiver would seem attractive at least to buy time, Housman has questioned whether it is likely to occur, since it "would, in effect, be asking the GATT parties who have repeatedly refused to join these environmental agreements to *de facto* join them in the form of the GATT's waiving in the rights and obligations contained in these agreements." See Housman, *Interaction*, pp. 7–8. See also Charnovitz, "GATT and the Environment," pp. 217–218.

23. Convention on International Trade in Endangered Species of Wild Flora and Fauna, March 3, 1973, 27 U.S.T. 1087, T.I.A.S. No. 8249, 993 U.N.T.S. 243.

24. Basel Convention on the Control of Transboundary Movements of Hazardous Wastes and Their Disposal, March 27, 1989, U.N. Doc. UNEP/I.G. 80/3 (1989), reprinted in I.L.M. vol. 28, p. 657.

25. See Jackson, "World Trade Rules," p. 1245 and annex B, p. 1271.

26. David Ricardo, *The Principles of Political Economy and Taxation* (1817), as quoted in Dunoff, "Reconciling International Trade," p. 1422.

27. The index of GDP at constant prices increased from a base of 100 in 1985 to 117.4 in 1990. See International Monetary Fund, *International Financial Statistical Yearbook* (Washington, D.C., 1992), p. 151. Environmental critics of such studies point out, consistent with the theoretical observations made in appendix A, that GDP per capita measures fail to account for environmental externalities, and that actual welfare gains may be overstated. See Michael D. Young, *Sustainable Investment and Resource Use: Equity, Environmental Integrity and Economic Efficiency* (Paris and Carnforth, Australia: UNESCO and the Parthenon Publishing Group, 1992).

28. See Nicholas Kaldor, "Welfare Propositions in Economics and Interpersonal Comparisons of Utility," *Economic Journal*, vol. 49 (September 1939), pp. 549–552, and John Hicks, "The Foundations of Welfare Economics," *Eco-*

nomic Journal, vol. 49 (December 1939), pp. 696–712. The authors described "compensation tests" in terms of a classic exercise in trade liberalization, the British corn laws, and asked whether losses to landlords in the value of land, if compensated, did not justify the policy of liberalizing trade. Hicks (p. 711) wrote: "Every simple economic reform inflicts a loss upon some people; the reforms we have studied are marked out by the characteristic that they will allow of compensation to balance that loss, and they will show a net advantage. Yet when such reforms have been carried through in historical fact, the advance has usually been amid the clash of opposing interests, so that compensation has not been given, and economic progress has accumulated a roll of victims sufficient to give all sound policy a bad name."

29. Joseph E. Stiglitz, "Information and Economic Analysis: A Perspective," *Economic Journal*, vol. 95 (Conference Papers Supplement, 1985), pp. 21–41. See also C. Ford Runge and Robert J. Myers, "Shifting Foundation of Agricultural Policy Analysis: Welfare Economics When Risk Markets Are Incomplete," *American Journal of Agricultural Economics*, vol. 67, no. 5 (December 1985), pp. 1010–1016.

30. Kym Anderson has developed a simple economic model of this interaction, which is presented in appendix A.

31. David Voigt, "The Maquiladora Problem in the Age of NAFTA: Where Will We Find Solutions?" *Minnesota Journal of Global Trade*, vol. 2, no. 2 (Summer 1993), p. 329.

32. See Ezra V. Mishan, "The Postwar Literature on Externalities: An Interpretive Essay," *Journal of Economic Literature*, vol. 9, no. 1 (March 1971), pp. 1–28. On the relation of trade to externalities, see John Whalley, "The Interface between Environmental and Trade Policies," *Economic Journal*, vol. 101, no. 405 (March 1991), pp. 180–189.

33. Carlo Perroni and Randall M. Wigle, "Modelling the Linkages Between International Trade and the Environment." (Waterloo, Ontario: Wilfrid Laurier University, 1992).

34. Some economists seem to imply that the preferences of developing countries (and, presumably, the individuals in those countries) for environmental improvements are different from those in the North, and that these countries' "absorptive capacity" for pollution or hazardous wastes is therefore greater. Whether true or not, this perspective has found little favor in either North or South, and appears to many as patronizing, if not neocolonial. A more empirically based observation is that developing countries simply lack the budgetary resources or political will to undertake the complex tasks represented by the Environmental Protection Agency or Occupational Safety and Health Administration in the United States and by similar agencies in other wealthy countries. See C. Ford Runge, "Trade Protectionism and Environmental Regulations: The New Nontariff Barriers," *Northwestern Journal of International Law and Business*, vol. 11, no. 1 (Spring 1990), pp. 47–61. Two Princeton economists have shown that as national incomes increase above a threshold of $5,000 per capita, environmental pollution (in this case, air pollution) begins to fall. This finding seems to confirm a link between levels of development and the environment, but as the authors acknowledge, the mechanism behind the linkage remains unexplained. See Gene Grossman and Alan

Kreuger, *Environmental Impacts of a North American Free Trade Agreement*, Woodrow Wilson School of Public Affairs Discussion Paper, no. 158 (Princeton, N.J., 1991).

35. Fundamentally, pollution and environmental degradation are forms of waste, analogous to heat loss in an engine. This thermodynamic perspective was first explored by the brilliant economic theorist Nicholas Georgescu-Roegen, in his technically complex and therefore widely unappreciated book *The Entropy Law and the Economic Process* (Cambridge, Mass.: Harvard University Press, 1971).

36. Kerry Krutilla, "Environmental Regulation in an Open Economy," *Journal of Environmental Economics and Management*, vol. 20 (1991), pp. 127–142. The targets and instruments distinction was first developed by Jan Tinbergen in *On the Theory of Economic Policy* (Amsterdam: Elsevier, North Holland, 1950).

37. Robert Repetto, *Trade and Environmental Policies: Achieving Complementarities and Avoiding Conflicts* (Washington, D.C.: World Resources Institute, 1993).

38. See David Robertson, "The Global Environment: Are International Treaties a Distraction?" *The World Economy*, vol. 13, no. 1 (March 1990), pp. 111–127.

CHAPTER 3

1. Prior to 1987 and the Single European Act, which established the legal foundation for EU environmental policy, the Treaty of Rome indirectly provided this justification. Article 100 provides for harmonizing laws that affect the functioning of the common market; article 235 permits the EU to take measures to attain objectives not expressly provided for elsewhere. See Commission of the EU, *European Community, Environmental Legislation*. Volume 1: *General Policy* (Luxembourg: Office of Official Publications, 1992). For a discussion of the origin and evolution of EU environmental policy, see Stanley P. Johnson and Guy Corcelle, *The Environmental Policy of the European Communities*, International Environmental Law and Policy Series (London: Graham and Trotman, 1989).

2. See U.S. Congress, OTA, *Trade and Environment: Conflicts and Opportunities* (Washington, D.C.: U.S. Government Printing Office, 1992). An excellent review is Amelia Porges, "Harmonization in the EU" (Geneva: Office of Legal Affairs, GATT Secretariat, 1993).

3. Charles S. Pearson, "Regional Free Trade and the Environment." (Paper for the IDB/ECLAC Project, Western Hemisphere Liberalization. The Paul H. Nitze School of Advanced International Studies, The Johns Hopkins University, October 1992.)

4. Ibid., p. 44; and Porges, "Harmonization," p. 8.

5. See Johnson and Corcelle, *Environmental Policy*, pp. 3–4, and p. 345. For a discussion of the unanimity rule, see C. Ford Runge and Harald von Witzke, "Institutional Change in the Common Agricultural Policy of the European Community," *American Journal of Agricultural Economics*, vol. 69, no. 2 (May 1987), pp. 213–222.

6. Pearson, "Regional Free Trade," p. 47.

7. Case 240/83 [1985] EUR 531, para. 15, quoted in Porges, "Harmonization," p. 14. The *Commission v. Italy* case reference is case 92/79 [1980] EUR 115.
8. See "Single Market: Double Standards (editorial)," *Eurofood: Food and Drink in the European Community* (April 1993), p. 1.
9. Pearson, "Regional Free Trade," p. 50; and *International Environmental Reporter*, April 10, 1991, p. 187.
10. Commission of the European Communities, Task Force on Environment and the Internal Market, *1992: The Environmental Dimension* (Bonn: Economica, Verlag, 1990). Konrad von Moltke, in reviewing this chapter, suggested that the task force was a "relatively academic exercise on the fringes of EU environmental policy." Its role, apart from establishing academic categories for analysis, was thus limited.
11. Konrad von Moltke, personal communication, August 16, 1993.
12. Food and Agriculture Organization (FAO), Policy Analysis Division, *Socio-economic Aspects of Environmental Policies in European Agriculture*. (Prepared for the Seventeenth Regional Conference for Europe, Venice, February, 1990).
13. Monika Hartmann and Alan Matthews, "Sustainable Agriculture in the European Community: The Role of Policy," *Forum for Applied Research and Public Policy*, vol. 8, 1993.
14. Ibid.
15. C. Ford Runge, *Environmental Effects of Trade in the Agricultural Sector*, Center for International Food and Agricultural Policy Working Paper, no. P92-1 (St. Paul: University of Minnesota, 1992). See also Courtney Harold and C. Ford Runge, "GATT and the Environment: Policy Research Needs," *American Journal of Agricultural Economics*, vol. 75 (August 1993), pp. 789–93.
16. Stephen L. Haley, *Environmental and Agricultural Policy Linkages in the European Community: The Nitrate Problem and CAP Reform*, International Agricultural Trade Research Consortium Working Paper, no. 93-3 (Washington, D.C.: April 1993), p. 2.
17. See Helmut Wulff, *Tapioca* (Frankfurt am Main: Verlag Alfred Strothe, 1987).
18. Hans-Joachim Winterling and Stefan Tangermann, *Economic Implications of Restricting Manioc Trade between Thailand and the EU* (Kiel: Wissenschaftsverlag Vauk, 1987).
19. The EU has similar agreements with Indonesia, China, and Vietnam. See K. D. Schumacher, "EC Supply Agreements for Tapioca," *Kraftfutter*, vol. 7 (1990), pp. 273–275. For a general discussion, see Kent Jones, "Voluntary Export Restraint: Political Economy, History and the Role of GATT," *Journal of World Trade*, vol. 23, no. 3 (1989), pp. 125–140. For an analysis of the footwear industry, see Carl B. Hamilton, Jaime de Melo, and L. Alan Winters, "Who Wins and Who Loses from Voluntary Export Restraints? The Case of Footwear," *World Bank Research Observer*, vol. 7, no. 1 (January 1992), pp. 17–33. The authors conclude that voluntary restraints "protect few jobs in the importing country (and then only temporarily), whereas their effects on employment and wages in the exporting countries are mainly negative—with highly inequitable consequences for income distribution, since workers in developing countries have considerably lower standards of living than either

130   FREER TRADE, PROTECTED ENVIRONMENT

capital owners in developing countries or workers in industrial countries" (p. 31).

20. See FAO, *Socioeconomic Aspects of Environmental Policies.*
21. Johannes B. Opschoor, "North-South Trade, Resource Degradation and Economic Security," *Bulletin of Peace Proposals*, vol. 20, no. 2 (1989), pp. 135–142.
22. Hartmann and Matthews, "Sustainable Agriculture," p. 3.
23. Ibid., p. 5.
24. Dale Leuck, "Policies to Reduce Nitrate Pollution in the European Community and Possible Effects on Livestock Production" (Washington, D.C.: U.S. Department of Agriculture, Economic Research Service, 1993).
25. Haley, *Environmental and Agricultural Policy Linkages*, pp. 19–25.
26. Task Force on Environment and the Internal Market, *1992: The Environmental Dimension.*
27. A *maquiladora* is a foreign-owned plant in Mexico subject to duty-free import of raw materials, in which finished products are exported duty-free except for value added in Mexico. See Malissa H. McKeith, "The Environment and Free Trade: Meeting Halfway at the Mexican Border," *Pacific Basin Law Journal*, vol. 10, no. 1 (1991), pp. 183–211.
28. Carla Hills, U.S. Trade Representative. (Presentation to the Senate Finance Committee Hearing, September 8, 1992). For a review of the environmental provisions of NAFTA, see Raymond Mikesell, "Analysis of the Provisions of the North American Free Trade Agreement of September 6, 1992." (Prepared for the Council on Foreign Relations Study Group on Trade and the Environment, Austin, Tex., January 14, 1993).
29. *Description of the Proposed North American Free Trade Agreement*, prepared by the governments of Canada, the United Mexican States, and the United States of America, August 12, 1992, p. 1.
30. Murray G. Smith, *Canadian Perspectives on Implementation of NAFTA* (Ottawa, Ontario: 1993), Center for Trade Policy and Law, Carleton University, p. 9.
31. Timothy J. Kehoe, "Assessing the Economic Impact of North American Free Trade," Discussion Paper no. 265, Center for Economic Research, Department of Economics, University of Minnesota, Minneapolis, October 1992, p. 6.
32. *Description of the Proposed North American Free Trade Agreement*, prepared by the governments of Canada, the United Mexican States, and the United States of America, August 12, 1992, p. 4.
33. Michael Scott Feeley and Elizabeth Knier, "Environmental Considerations of the Emerging United States–Mexico Free Trade Agreement, 2," *Duke Journal of Comparative and International Law*, vol. 2, no. 2 (1992), p. 272, cited in David Voigt, "The Maquiladora Problem in the Age of NAFTA: Where Will We Find Solutions?" *Minnesota Journal of Global Trade*, vol. 2, no. 2 (1993), p. 328.
34. Paul Salopek, "Crowded Border Imports High Rate of Disease: Maquilas Bring Workers, but Sewage, Health Systems Aren't Ready," *El Paso Times*, May 14, 1991, p. 1A.
35. United States General Accounting Office, *North American Free Trade Agreement, U.S.-Mexico Trade and Investment Data*, GAO/GGD-92-131 (Washington, D.C., 1992), p. 9.

NOTES

131

36. John Maggs, "G.M. to Treat Sewage at 35 Mexican Factories," *Austin American-Statesman*, May 15, 1991.
37. Gaynell Terrell, "Tragic Puzzle Grips Families on the Border: Plant Pollution May Cause Brain Not to Develop," *Houston Post*, May 17, 1991, p. A1.
38. Treaties and Other International Acts Series (T.I.A.S.), no. 1027. Reprinted at I.L.M., vol. 22, p. 1025 (1983).
39. Jan Gilbreath and J. Ben Tonra, *Environment: Unwelcome Guest at the Free Trade Party*, Center for Strategic and International Studies (CSIS) Policy Papers on the Americas, vol. 3, no. 10 (Washington, D.C.: 1992), p. 24.
40. Peter M. Emerson, Environmental Defense Fund, personal communication, January 15, 1993.
41. Peter M. Emerson and Elizabeth Wallace Bourbon, "The Border Environment and Free Trade." (Prepared for the North American Institute, Santa Fe, November 8, 1991, p. 11.)
42. David Voigt, "The Maquiladora Problem in the Age of NAFTA: Where Will We Find Solutions?" *Minnesota Journal of Global Trade*, vol. 2, no. 2 (1993), pp. 300–336.
43. Gilbreath and Tonra, *Environment*, p. 23.
44. Voigt, "The Maquiladora Problem." SEDESOL is the successor agency to the Secretariat of Urban Development (SEDUE) and assumed responsibility for the environmental functions of SEDUE on May 26, 1992.
45. Gilbreath and Tonra, *Environment*, p. 27.
46. Ibid., p. 36.
47. Susan McAtee Monday, "Toxins Found in Border Ditch Pose Serious Health Threat," *San Antonio Light*, November 12, 1991, p. 1A.
48. Gilbreath and Tonra, *Environment*, p. 34.
49. Ibid., p. 28.
50. Judith M. Dean, "Trade and the Environment: A Survey of the Literature," in Patrick Low, ed., *International Trade and the Environment*, World Bank Discussion Papers, no. 159 (Washington, D.C., 1992), p. 27.
51. James A. Tobey, "The Effects of Domestic Environmental Policies on Patterns of World Trade: An Empirical Test," *Kyklos*, vol. 43, no. 2 (1990), pp. 193–194.
52. Patrick Low, "Trade Measures and Environmental Quality: The Implication for Mexico's Exports" (draft, 1991), annex table A, cited in Gary C. Hufbauer and Jeffrey J. Schott, *North American Free Trade: Issues and Recommendations* (Washington, D.C.: Institute for International Economics, 1992), p. 150.
53. Gilbreath and Tonra, *Environment*, p. 35.
54. Ibid., p. 35.
55. Local, transnational, and global externalities are discussed in chapter 2.
56. The two pesticide effects presented here can also be categorized under *product effects* or *process effects* (see the discussion of the tuna-dolphin dispute in chapter 4). In the case of pesticide residues, the product effects are the pesticide effects that remain with the product, such as the pesticide residues; the process effect is the harmful effects of pesticide on the environment at the point where crop production occurs. While obvious for agricultural products, this distinction does not generalize easily to all processes and final products. Nor do product and process effects necessarily correspond to transnational and local externalities, as in this case.

57. For some of the specific proposals advanced, see Stewart J. Hudson and Rodrigo J. Prudencio (for the National Wildlife Federation), "The North American Commission on Environment and Other Supplemental Environmental Agreements: Part Two of the NAFTA Package," February 4, 1993; Justin Ward and S. Jacob Scherr (for the Natural Resources Defense Council), "Environmental Elements of the NAFTA Package: Testimony of the Natural Resources Defense Council before the Committee on Environment and Public Works, U.S. Senate," March 16, 1993; and J. Michael McCloskey and John Audley (for the Sierra Club), "Environmental Concerns Regarding the North American Free Trade Agreement," February 1993. See also Steve Charnovitz, "NAFTA: An Analysis of Its Environmental Provisions," *Environmental Law Reporter*, vol. 23 (February 1993), pp. 10067–73.
58. See Scott Otteman, "Special Report: Near Final NAFTA Greens Text Narrows Scope of Original U.S. Proposal," *Inside U.S. Trade*, vol. 11, no. 33 (August 20, 1993), p. 1.
59. NAFTA article 755.5 discusses participation in international standardizing bodies; article 756 discusses the role of "equivalence" versus strict harmonization; and article 762 discusses technical cooperation in standard setting. Articles 906.1 and 906.2 commit the parties to seek compatible environmental standards, and annexes 913-A and 913-C establish subcommittees to set emissions and air quality standards, among other things. Article 1114.2 commits the parties to avoid lowering or failing to enforce standards as a means of attracting investment.
60. Cited in Ward, "Environmental Elements," p. 4. See also testimony of Ambassador Mickey Kantor, U.S. Trade Representative, before the Senate Committee on Finance, March 9, 1993, and the House Ways and Means Subcommittee on International Trade, March 11, 1993; and George Foy, "Environmental Protection versus Intellectual Property: The U.S.-Mexico Free Trade Agreement Negotiation," *International Environmental Affairs*, vol. 4 (Fall 1992), pp. 323–337.
61. Office of the U.S. Trade Representative, *NAFTA Supplemental: Agreement on Environmental Cooperation* (Washington, D.C., 1993).
62. Otteman, "Special Report," n. 32, and accompanying text of draft side agreement.
63. See McCloskey and Audley, "Environmental Concerns," n. 31, p. iii.
64. The polluter-pays principle is essentially an application of conventional economic prescriptions to "internalize" negative externalities by levying a fee or charge on firms or industries responsible for the pollution. It is endorsed as environmental policy by the OECD.

CHAPTER 4

1. "United States—Restrictions on Imports of Tuna." GATT Doc. No. DS21/R September 3, 1991.
2. Public Law 92-522, as amended by Public laws 100-711 and 101-627. Codified as 16 U.S.C. 1371. Implementing regulations are at 50 C.F.R. Part 216, and for commercial fleets at 50 C.F.R 216.24.

3. Eli Whitney Debevoise II, personal communication, September 14, 1992. On December 2, 1992, the United States lifted the secondary embargo on France. As of February 1993 the countries subject to secondary embargoes were Costa Rica, Italy, Japan, and Spain. Primary embargoes applied at that date to Colombia, Mexico, and Venezuela.

4. Mexico argued that the MMPA was inconsistent with GATT articles III (national treatment), XI (prohibiting quantitative import barriers), and XIII (requiring nondiscriminatory application of quantitative restrictions).

5. As discussed in chapter 2, article XX(b) refers to exceptions to the GATT articles that authorize measures "necessary to protect human, animal, or plant life or health"; article XX(g) refers to measures "relating to the conservation of exhaustible natural resources if such measures are made effective in conjunction with restrictions on domestic production or consumption."

6. The panel reached essentially the same conclusions regarding the secondary embargo provisions of the MMPA. It also found that the exceptions relating to the conservation of exhaustible natural resources under article XX(g) did not extend to extrajurisdictional conservation, and that since the "1.25 times" ratio could be a large or small number (depending on the U.S. catch), the MMPA was not "primarily aimed at the conservation of dolphins."

7. GATT, *International Trade 90–91*, vol. 1 (Geneva, 1992), pp. 19–39.

8. The Packwood Amendment to the Magnuson Fishery Conservation and Management Act, 16 USC 1821(e)(2); and the Pelly Amendment to the Fishermen's Protective Act of 1967, 22 USC 1978.

9. 16 USC 420.

10. C.F.R. pt. 82, promulgated under the Clean Air Act, section 601–618. 72 USC 7671-7671 q.

11. John H. Jackson, "World Trade Rules and Environmental Policies: Congruence or Conflict?" *Washington and Lee Law Review*, vol. 49, no. 4 (Fall 1992), appendix B, p. 1273.

12. "United States—Restrictions on Imports of Tuna," para. 5.28, p. 1620.

13. This language is based on the Report of the GATT Panel, United States section 337 of the Tariff Act of 1930, para. 5.26 (November 7, 1989), B/SD 36th Supp. 345, 392–393. While it referred there to article XX(d), it was used to refer to article XX(b) by the GATT Dispute Settlement Panel Report on Thai Restrictions on Importation of and Internal Taxes on Cigarettes, para. 73, I.L.M., vol. 30 (1991), p. 1122.

14. Steve Charnovitz, "GATT and the Environment: Examining the Issues," *International Environmental Affairs*, vol. 4, no. 3 (Summer 1992), pp. 203–233.

15. "United States—Restrictions on Imports of Tuna," para. 5.33, p. 1621.

16. Eli Whitney Debevoise II, personal communication, November 17, 1992.

17. See Jeffrey L. Dunoff, "Reconciling International Trade with Preservation of the Global Commons: Can We Prosper and Protect?" *Washington and Lee Law Review*, vol. 49, no. 4 (Fall 1992), pp. 1407–1454.

18. Eli Whitney Debevoise II, personal communication. November 17, 1992; and Robert Hudec, personal communication, March 5, 1993.

19. One of these panel reports, "Canada—Measures Affecting Exports of Unprocessed Herring and Salmon," is discussed later in this chapter. See U.S. Congress, OTA, *Trade and Environment: Conflicts and Opportunities* (Wash-

ington, D.C.: U.S. Government Printing Office, May 1992), p. 49, n. 49. See also Pierre Pescatore et al., *Handbook of GATT Dispute Settlement* (Ardsley-on-Hudson, N.Y.: Transnational Juris Publications, 1991).

20. "United States—Restrictions on Imports of Tuna." paras. 26 and 31, cited in OTA, *Trade and Environment*, pp. 49–50.

21. Charnovitz, "GATT and the Environment," pp. 208–209, notes that "extra-jurisdictionality" is not the same as "extraterritoriality," such as when U.S. laws are applied to domestic firms in foreign countries to regulate technology transfer, corrupt practices, and trading with the enemy.

22. Dunoff, "Reconciling International Trade." See also Steve Charnovitz, "Exploring the Environmental Exceptions in GATT Article XX," *Journal of World Trade Law*, vol. 25, no. 2 (October 1991), p. 37. Konrad von Moltke (personal communication, August 16, 1992) notes that article 36 of the European Economic Community Treaties grows out of the same tradition as GATT article XX, but has led to a different history of interpretation.

23. Charnovitz, "GATT and the Environment," p. 209. Jackson, "World Trade Rules," pp. 1241–1242, has noted that while Charnovitz's views are "interesting," they "are not entirely persuasive," and that Charnovitz "overlooks important issues of treaty interpretation." Jackson states:

> Under typical international law, elaborated by the Vienna Convention on the Law of Treaties, preparatory work history is an ancillary means of interpreting treaties. In the context of interpreting the GATT, we have more than forty years of practice since the origin of GATT, and we also have some very important policy questions raised by the "slippery slope arguments." . . . Thus, unlike certain schools of thought concerning United States Supreme Court interpretation of the United States Constitution, it is this author's view that one cannot rely too heavily on the original drafting history.

24. Joseph Greenwald, as cited in Charnovitz, "GATT and the Environment," n. 56.

25. Laura L. Lones, "The Marine Mammal Protection Act and International Protection of Cetaceans: A Unilateral Attempt to Effectuate Transnational Conservation," *Vanderbilt Journal of Transnational Law*, vol. 22, no. 4 (1989); see pp. 997–1017. From a historical perspective, the draft of article XX(g) also appears to exist to protect international fish and wildlife agreements. If the drafters felt strongly about such agreements respecting article XX(b), then presumably the same view prevailed toward article XX(g). See Charnovitz, "GATT and the Environment," p. 210. Referring to article XX(g), in contrast to article XX(b), Charnovitz notes that "in considering its scope, there is no reason to presume that the drafters were environmentally cosmopolitan in one part of the ITO Charter and environmentally nativistic in another."

26. In addition to this reliance on GATT article III, the U.S. case relied on the note to article III, which states in part:

> Any internal tax . . . or any law, regulation or requirement of the kind referred to in [article III, para. 1] which applies to an imported product and the like domestic product and is collected or

enforced in the case of the imported product at the time or point of importation, is . . . subject to the provisions of article III.

27. Dunoff, "Reconciling International Trade," p. 1414.
28. GATT, *International Trade 90–91*, pp. 19–39.
29. Jackson, "World Trade Rules," p. 1243.
30. Ibid., p. 1244.
31. See D.W. Bromley, ed., *Making the Commons Work: Theory, Practice and Policy* (San Francisco: Institute for Contemporary Studies Press, 1992).
32. Catch estimates are obtained through radio communications with fishing boats (hails), and with harvesters and tenders collecting harvests from the vessels. Landing stations report catch estimates by species, weight, and number, and are subject to inspections by fisheries officials. These methods, combined with biological sampling on the fishing grounds and at landing sites, form the data base for restrictive fishing policies.
33. Article XX becomes relevant only after a measure is first found in violation of GATT's general rules.
34. U.S.-Canada Binational Panel Final Report, ITRD vol. 12 (Oct. 16, 1989), pp. 1026–44.
35. U.S.-Canada Binational Panel Final Report, para. 7.08–7.09, p. 1036 (emphasis added).
36. Article 407, entitled "Import and Export Restrictions," provides: "Subject to the further rights and obligations of this Agreement, the Parties affirm their respective rights and obligations under the General Agreement on Tariffs and Trade (GATT) with respect to prohibitions or restrictions on bilateral trade in goods" (para. 1).
37. U.S.-Canada Binational Panel Final Report, para. 6.04, p. 1032.
38. U.S.-Canada Binational Panel Final Report, para. 6.12, p. 1034.
39. "Canada—Measures Affecting Exports of Unprocessed Herring and Salmon," L/6268 (November 1987), para. 4.6; quoted in the U.S.-Canada Binational Panel Final Report, para. 7.04, p. 1035.
40. The panel referred to the prohibition against disguised restrictions in the preamble of article XX as "just the opposite face" of the argument in article XX(g) that the measures must have a "true conservation purpose."
41. U.S.-Canada Binational Panel Final Report, para. 7.05, p. 1036.
42. U.S.-Canada Binational Panel Final Report, para. 7.07, p. 1036.
43. U.S.-Canada Binational Panel Final Report, para. 6.09, p. 1033. The panel cites two other GATT panel rulings in support: Japan—Customs Duties, Taxes and Labeling Practices on Imported Wines and Alcoholic Beverages, L/6216, BISD, 34th Supp., p. 83 (1987), para. 5.10–5.11; and United States—Taxes on Petroleum and Certain Imported Substances, L/6175, BISD 34th Supp., p. 136 (1987), para. 5.1.9.
44. See A. Myrick Freeman, Robert H. Havemen, and Allen V. Kneese, *The Economics of Environmental Policy* (Malabar, Fla.: R. E. Krieger, 1984); John A. Siden and Albert C. Worrell, *Unpriced Values: Decisions without Market Prices* (New York: Wiley), 1979; and V. Kerry Smith, "Nonmarket Valuation of Environmental Resources: An Interpretive Appraisal," *Land Economics*, vol. 69, no. 1 (February 1993), pp. 1–26.
45. U.S.-Canada Binational Panel Final Report, para. 7.09–7.10, pp. 1036–1037.
46. U.S.-Canada Binational Panel Final Report, para. 7.40, p. 1043.

CHAPTER 5

1. Andrew Hurrell and Benedict Kingsbury, "The International Politics of the Environment: An Introduction," in Andrew Hurrell and Benedict Kingsbury, eds., *The International Politics of the Environment: Actors, Interests, and Institutions* (Oxford: Clarendon Press, 1992), p. 10, n. 20. See United Nations Environment Programme, *Register of Treaties and Other Agreements in the Field of the Environment* (Nairobi, 1991).
2. David W. Pearce and R. Kerry Turner, *Economics of Natural Resources and the Environment* (Baltimore: Johns Hopkins University Press, 1992), p. 199.
3. Vienna Convention for the Protection of the Ozone Layer 1985, I.L.M., vol. 26 (1987), p. 1516.
4. Montreal Protocol on Substances that Deplete the Ozone Layer 1987, I.L.M., vol. 26 (1987), p. 1541. For London Amendments, see Barry E. Carter and Phillip R. Trimble, eds., *International Law: Selected Documents* (Boston: Little, Brown & Co., 1991), p. 731.
5. Adjustments require a two-thirds majority and, under the 1987 Protocol, must include at least 50 percent of the total consumption of the controlled substance. Under the 1990 London Amendments, the two-thirds majority must include a majority of developing countries (defined in article 5) *and* a majority of nondeveloping countries.
6. These substances include CFCs, halons, carbon tetrachloride, methyl chloroform, and halogenated CFCs.
7. Hurrell and Kingsbury, "International Politics," pp. 17–18. See also Jamison Koehler and Scott A. Hajost, "The Montreal Protocol: A Dynamic Agreement for Protecting the Ozone Layer," *Ambio*, vol. 20 (1991), pp. 82–86.
8. U.S. Congress, OTA, *Trade and Environment: Conflicts and Opportunities* (Washington, D.C.: U.S. Government Printing Office, 1992), p. 42.
9. Ibid., pp. 44–45.

CHAPTER 6

1. Steve Charnovitz, "The Environment versus Trade Rules: Defogging the Debate," *Environmental Law*, vol. 23 (1993), pp. 481–482.
2. John H. Jackson, *World Trade and the Law of GATT* (New York: Bobbs Merrill, 1969), pp. 42–57. For an analysis of the ITO, see William Diebold, *The End of the ITO*, Princeton Essays in International Finance, no. 16 (Princeton, N.J., 1952).
3. I am indebted to Konrad von Moltke for proposing this institutional characterization of such a multilateral body (personal communication).
4. Those originally proposing an environment commission included the World Wildlife Fund (WWF), the National Wildlife Federation (NWF), the National Audubon Society (NAS), the Environmental Defense Fund (EDF), the Nature Conservancy, Defenders of Wildlife, and the Natural Resources Defense Council (NRDC). They were joined in a slightly amended proposal by the Center for International Environmental Law. On September 14, 1993, the WWF, NWF, NRDC, NAS, and EDF were joined by Conservation International in calling

explicitly for passage of NAFTA, together with its side agreements. Some groups remained opposed, including the Sierra Club, Public Citizen, Friends of the Earth, and Greenpeace. See Keith Schneider, "Environmentalists Fight Each Other over Trade Accord," *New York Times*, September 16, 1993, p. A1.

5. Justin R. Ward and Lynn M. Fischer, "An Agenda for the Environment: Priorities for NAFTA and Beyond," *Harvard Journal of World Affairs*, vol. 2 (Spring 1993), pp. 15–27.

6. U.S. General Accounting Office, *U.S.-Mexico Trade: Assessment of Mexico's Environmental Controls for New Companies* (Washington, D.C., 1992), p. 13.

7. The Global Environmental Facility was launched in 1991 as a three-year pilot program to allow for actions where no international agreement had yet been negotiated. It is jointly managed by the World Bank, the United Nations Environment Programme, and the United Nations Development Programme. Its role was further elaborated at the 1992 Rio Conference, and it has complex links to the Biodiversity and Climate Conventions, as well as to the Montreal Protocol. Its further role is, however, still the subject of debate among all of the organizations involved. See Kenneth Piddington, "The Role of the World Bank," in Andrew Hurrell and Benedict Kingsbury, eds., *The International Politics of the Environment: Actors, Interests and Institutions* (Oxford: Clarendon Press, 1992), p. 212–227.

8. For a discussion of the role of the UN agencies in global environmental affairs, see Peter S. Thacher, "The Role of the United Nations," in Hurrell and Kingsbury, *International Politics*, pp. 183–211. A cautionary note on the need for new institutions in the context of NAFTA is given in Stephen P. Mumme, "New Directions in United States–Mexican Transboundary Environmental Management: A Critique of Current Proposals," *Natural Resources Journal*, vol. 32 (Summer 1992), pp. 539–562. A proposal similar to that of the WEO is advanced by Dan Esty in "GATTing the Greens," *Foreign Affairs*, vol. 72, no. 5 (Nov./Dec. 1993), pp. 132–36.

9. Richardson's analysis and call for a Multilateral Environmental Agency is developed in the context of climate change, although the arguments he advances are general ones. See Elliot L. Richardson, "Climate Change: Problems of Law-Making," in Hurrell and Kingsbury, *International Politics*, pp. 166–182.

10. See Barbara J. Bramble and Gareth Porter, "Non-Governmental Organizations and the Making of U.S. International Environmental Policy," in Hurrell and Kingsbury, *International Politics*, pp. 313–353. See also Nancy Lindboug, "Non-Governmental Organizations: Their Past, Present and Future Role in International Environmental Negotiations," in Lawrence E. Susskind, Eric Jay Dolin, and J. William Breslin, eds., *International Environmental Treaty Making* (Cambridge, Mass.: Harvard University Program on Negotiation Books, 1992).

11. Richardson, "Climate Change," pp. 176–177.

12. Lawrence Susskind and Connie Ozawa, "Negotiating More Effective International Environmental Agreements," in Hurrell and Kingsbury, *International Politics*, pp. 110–141. See also Scott Barrett, "International Agreements for the Protection of Environmental and Agricultural Resources: An Economics Perspective" (London: London Business School, 1992).

13. Charnovitz has proposed modeling an International Environmental Organization on the International Labour Organization. See Charnovitz, "Environment versus Trade Rules," pp. 511–517.

14. For an analysis of "activist secretariats," with representation from nongovernmental organizations, see Rosemary Sandford, "Secretariats and International Environmental Negotiations: Two New Models," in Susskind et al., *International Environmental Treaty Making.*

15. Geza Feketekuty, "The Link between Trade and Environmental Policy," *Minnesota Journal of Global Trade*, vol. 2, no. 2 (Summer 1993), pp. 199–200. See also Betsy Baker, "Protection, Not Protectionism: Multilateral Environmental Agreements and the GATT," *Vanderbilt Journal of Transnational Law*, vol. 26, no. 3 (October 1993), pp. 437–68.

16. See Charnovitz, "Environment versus Trade Rules," pp. 513–514, and Steve Charnovitz, "Environmentalism Confronts GATT Rules—Recent Developments and New Opportunities," *Journal of World Trade*, vol. 27, no. 2 (April 1993), pp. 37–53.

17. Jessica Tuchman Mathews, "Redefining Security," *Foreign Affairs*, vol. 68, no. 2 (Spring 1989), pp. 162–177.

18. For a suggestion to tie food aid to environmental improvements, see Orville L. Freeman, "Perspectives and Prospects," *Agricultural History*, vol. 66, no. 2 (Spring 1992), pp. 3–11. For a more general analysis, see Robert Repetto, *Trade and Environmental Policies: Achieving Complementarities and Avoiding Conflicts* (Washington, D.C.: World Resources Institute, 1993).

19. For an informed and optimistic view of the new Europe, see Axel Krause, *Inside the New Europe* (New York: HarperCollins, 1991).

20. Nor, it should be noted, did the United States appear to do so during the 1992 Rio Conference. While expressing certain valid reservations, the U.S. stance was generally ill prepared and poorly executed, leaving a distinct impression of absent leadership.

21. Albert Gore, *Earth in the Balance: Ecology and the Human Spirit* (Boston: Houghton Mifflin, 1992).

APPENDIX A

1. This appendix is based in part on Kym Anderson, "Effects on the Environment and Welfare of Liberalizing World Trade: The Cases of Coal and Food," in Kym Anderson and Richard Blackhurst, eds., *The Greening of World Trade Issues* (Ann Arbor, Mich.: University of Michigan Press, 1992), pp. 145–172; and Kym Anderson, "The Standard Welfare Economics of Policies Affecting Trade and the Environment," ibid., pp. 25–48. I benefited from helpful discussions during its preparation with Kym Anderson and Richard Blackhurst of the GATT Secretariat, Division of Economic Research and Analysis, Geneva.

2. In addition to standard externalities theory, the assumptions underlying the model include the usual ones of partial equilibrium analysis in a trade setting. For the latter, see James P. Houck, *The Elements of Agricultural Trade Policies* (New York: Macmillan, 1986). The approach is sufficient for clarifying analytical issues of relevance to public and environmental policy, although it is

NOTES 139

subject to criticism by advocates of general equilibrium analysis. For example, see Michael Hazilla and Raymond J. Kopp, "Social Cost of Environmental Quality Regulations: A General Equilibrium Analysis," *Journal of Political Economy*, vol. 98, no. 4 (1990), pp. 853–873; and John D. Merrifield, "The Impact of Selected Abatement Strategies on Transnational Pollution, the Terms of Trade, and Factor Rewards: A General Equilibrium Approach," *Journal of Environmental Economics and Management*, vol. 15 (1988), pp. 259–284. Among the key underlying assumptions are that transaction costs prevent spontaneous negotiated "internalization" of the external effect, ruling out a market solution; that taxes-cum-subsidies are lump sum (nondistorting); that the externality can be accurately measured; that it is a product, rather than process, externality; that all curves are linear; that the externality begins with the first unit of production; and that the marginal benefit and cost curves fully incorporate feedback effects from the rest of the economy. See Kym Anderson, "Standard Welfare Economics."

3. John B. Sullivan, Jr., Melissa Gonzales, Gary R. Krieger, and C. Ford Runge, "Health Related Hazards of Agriculture," in John B. Sullivan, Jr., and Gary R. Krieger, eds., *Hazardous Materials Toxicology, Clinical Principles of Environmental Health* (Baltimore, Md.: Williams & Wilkins, 1992), pp. 642–646.

4. The empirical use of consumer and producer surplus measures is itself fraught with difficulty. See Robin W. Boadway and Neil Bruce, *Welfare Economics*, (New York: Basil Blackwell, 1984).

5. See Peter J. Lloyd, "The Problem of Optimal Environmental Policy Choice," in Anderson and Blackhurst, *The Greening of World Trade Issues*, pp. 49–72. The "equivalence" of these measures is, of course, not guaranteed in practice, as discussed in William J. Baumol and Wallace E. Oates. *The Theory of Environmental Policy: Externalities, Public Outlays, and the Quality of Life.* (Englewood Cliffs, N.J.: Prentice-Hall, 1975). In our example, the effect of such a policy would be to eliminate the "wedge" between S' and S, so that marginal social costs of production would equal marginal social benefits. In the case of no trade, such intervention would be equivalent to a tax of cn per unit, which would reduce corn production from OQ to OQ_0. The welfare benefit from internalizing the externality would be the shaded area cde, because of the reduced erosion resulting from the production fall. From a welfare perspective, we can thus isolate a welfare improvement due to the "environmental effect," of targeted environmental intervention, assuming no "liberalization effect."

6. Anderson, "Standard Welfare Economics," especially p. 28. What of the behavior of other trading nations in the world? Suppose that a large trading partner of the small country were to liberalize its agricultural trade in corn or undertake environmental policies designed to reduce soil erosion as well? In this case, either the "liberalization effect" or the "environmental effect" on welfare could occur in tandem in both countries. The effect on the small country of either more liberal trade or increased environmental intervention (and reduced production) in the large country would be to raise corn prices. If the international price of corn rose from OP, to OP''_1 in Figure A-1(b), the "liberalization effect" would rise from cij to cwx, or by $iwxj$, given an environ-

mental intervention that raised the equivalent tax on erosion from js to xl. But if no such environmental policies were taken, gains from the "liberalization effect" ($ikyw$) would be reduced by the losses from erosion ($mkyz$), which might be a net gain or loss, depending on both the increase in price and, more important, how great the divergence was between S and S'—in other words, how serious the impact of erosion on welfare.

Index

141

OTA (Office of Technology Assessment), 77, 92
Oversight reports, 68
Ozawa, Connie, 104
Ozone depletion, 4, 12, 13, 19–21, 25–26; and CFCs (chlorofluorocarbons), 25, 30, 89–91; and the "later in time" rule, 20–21; and the Montreal Protocol, 7, 20–21, 74, 88–93, 98, 105
Packwood Amendment, 74
Pelly Amendment, 74
Perot, Ross, 4
Pesticides, 30, 41, 46, 65–66
Petroleum fuel, 24–25, 28
"Polluter pays" principle, 70
"Pollution havens," 34, 54, 64–65, 69
Portugal, 35, 55
Presidential campaigns (United States), 4, 55
Price levels, 40, 41, 48, 49, 113
"Primarily aimed at" test, 16, 18–19, 68, 78, 81–86, 93
Principles: "polluter pays" principle, 70; subsidiarity principle, 36–37, 38, 52, 70, 96, 99
Process bans, 73, 79–80
Procureur de la République v. Association de Défense des Bruleurs d'Huiles Usagées, 37
Product-process distinctions, 73, 79–80, 97, 131n56
"Proportionality" test, 16, 19
Protectionism, 3, 11, 19, 74–75; and abstract arguments favoring free trade, 22; and cross-border taxes, 70; "disguised," 7, 14, 38, 71, 74, 97; and the EU, 35, 36, 38, 40, 52; and national treatment, 15; and welfare gains, 24
Public Citizen, 1, 13

Radiation, ultraviolet, 90
Recognition, mutual, doctrine of, 36–37
Ricardo, David, 22

Richardson, Elliot L., 103–4
Rio Conference (1992), 26, 69, 88, 95, 103, 108–9

Salinas de Gortari, Carlos, 54–55, 63, 64
Salmon-herring dispute, 29, 71, 80–86, 97–98, 103; and benefits and costs, 85; and the "primarily aimed at" test, 18–19, 81, 82–85, 86, 93
Sanctions, 68, 76. *See also* Embargoes
Scale effects, 34
SEDESOL (Secretariat of Social Development), 63, 64
Sierra Club, 1, 3, 13
Single European Act, 36–38
Skin disease, 90
Smith, Adam, 22
Soil contamination, 40–42, 44, 48–49
Sovereignty, 68
Soviet Union, 103
Spain, 35, 55
Spatial effects, 38–39
Species reduction, 21–22, 41, 43, 45, 74
Standards of living, 2
Static effects, 38–39, 41
Subsidiarity principle, 36–37, 38, 52, 70, 96, 99
Subsidies, 12, 40
Sulfur dioxide, 26
Superfund (United States), 25
Susskind, Lawrence, 104

Targets, trade, 29–32, 68, 93
Taxes, 12, 32, 113; cross-border, 70; and the EU, 40; and externalities, 25, 28
Tests: disguised restriction, 16, 19; necessity, 16, 18, 75, 83, 84; primarily aimed at, 16, 18–19, 68, 78, 81–86, 93; proportionality, 16, 19
Texas, 62